PERIL IN PARADISE

Theology, Science, and the Age of the Earth

PERIL IN
PARADISE

Theology, Science, and the Age of the Earth

Mark S. Whorton, Ph.D

Authentic

Authentic Media
We welcome your comments and questions.
129 Mobilization Drive, Waynesboro, GA 30830 USA authentic@stl.org
and 9 Holdom Avenue, Bletchley, Milton Keynes, Bucks, MK1 1QR, UK
www.authenticbooks.com

If you would like a copy of our current catalog, contact us at:
1-8MORE-BOOKS
ordersusa@stl.org

Peril in Paradise
ISBN: 1-932805-23-0

Copyright © 2005 by Mark Whorton

10 09 08 07 06 05 / 6 5 4 3 2 1

Cover design: Paul Lewis
Interior design: Angela Duerksen
Editorial team: Dave Albertson, KJ Larson

Printed in the United States of America

For thinking believers
and
believing thinkers

CONTENTS

PREFACE

"... it seemed fitting for me as well, having investigated
everything carefully from the beginning, to write *it* out for you ...
**so that you might know the exact truth about the
things you have been taught."(Luke 1:3–4)**

There is no lack of books that take a side and make a case for
the age of the earth. Many excellent books are available that dig
into nuances of Hebrew and esoteric scientific principles. There
is, however, one important perspective missing, and that is the big
picture. Why do Christians divide themselves so strongly on the
issue of science and faith? Why do we "Bible-believers" oppose
each other with animosity and heated rhetoric when it comes to
the first three chapters of the Bible? The answer can be boiled
down to one issue with far-reaching implications: the age of the
earth—the line of demarcation that divides us into two camps with
fundamentally different theological worldviews.

Far beyond time, the young-earth and old-earth creation
camps are built on two very different theological frameworks.
Essentially the difference boils down to two small words: "very
good." What did the Creator mean when He pronounced His cre-

ation very good? This question bears directly on the philosophical problem of pain and suffering, the proper role of redemption, the nature of end times, and the ultimate reason we were created. How one treats the age of the earth impacts virtually every major Christian doctrine.

Plain and simple, my goal in writing this book is *"so that you might know the exact truth about the things you have been taught"* (Luke 1:4).

As followers of Christ we must first and foremost be committed to a pursuit of truth. With this in mind, this book systematically examines the theological foundations of young-earth and old-earth views to determine which creation paradigm most accurately represents the truth that God has revealed.

Along the way I have had considerable help with my goal. I am deeply indebted to Hill Roberts for his critique of an early draft and his knowledgeable and insightful input as the book developed. Dr. Ray Bohlin of Probe Ministries helped clarify and sharpen my reasoning while maintaining what I hope is a fair treatment with a consistently gracious tone. Other substantive contributions came from Krista Bontrager, Dr. Don Atkinson, Dr. Jimmy Jackson, Jeff Yeager, Harold McDaniel, John Walley, Paul Elbert, and Dr. David Hampton who reviewed various parts of the manuscript. Special thanks go to Volney James, Angela Duerksen, and my editor Dave Albertson at Authentic Media/Paternoster who have been excellent to work with.

PART 1

A HOUSE DIVIDED

THE BATTLE LINES ARE DRAWN 1

It turned out to be a good day for running late. This particular Monday morning Lee missed the opening assembly for the Ladies' Bible study. When she arrived, her friends were still drinking coffee and talking about some troublemakers in the church.

During the opening assembly, Dr. Alice McLynn, the Women's ministry leader, asked the women to pray about something that happened during a class she had taught the night before. Two men who evidently did not believe in the authority of the Bible had disrupted her class. To make matters worse, these men were teachers in the church. Dr. McLynn told the women, "We have to be on our guard for people who compromise the clear truth of God's Word. The Devil attacks the church through people who do not respect the authority of God's Word."

As Lee sat down, she overheard one of her friends say, "Can you believe that someone in our church is teaching heresy?"

"How could anyone be a teacher in our church and not believe the gospel?" another asked.

Not knowing that she had missed the opening assembly, one friend turned to her and asked, "Do you have any idea who

Dr. McLynn was talking about?" My wife started to cringe because she knew the answer. I was one of the heretics.

The Spark

The topic of Dr. McLynn's "Science and the Bible" class on the previous night had been scientific evidence that the earth was created between 6,000 and 10,000 years ago. Not wanting to disrupt the class, a friend and I waited until the class ended to ask her to clarify one of her comments. I was careful to ask my questions gingerly knowing that the issue was a powder keg, but simply asking questions was enough to strike the spark.

My question to Dr. McLynn was about one of her arguments for a young earth, and the conversation quickly turned to the length of days during the creation week. She emphatically stated that the days in the creation account of Genesis could not mean anything other than regular, twenty-four-hour days. Knowing that not all Old Testament scholars agree with her, I asked her, "Is it not possible that Moses was talking about longer periods than regular solar days?"

"Well perhaps," she responded, "but the real problem with an ancient creation is not the meaning of the Hebrew words as much as the compromise of biblical authority."

This is the spark that ignited the controversy and alerted her to the heretics in her class.

The Silver Bullet

Dr. McLynn shifted gears and carefully stated her deeper problem with an old earth. "How could there be millions of years of suffering in the world before man was on the scene to mess up God's perfect creation? You simply cannot believe the Bible and believe in an ancient creation. Old earth creation is a compromise of biblical authority that insults the character of God and even threatens the gospel of Christ!"

Here was the rub. If the earth really is billions of years old, then there were hurricanes, hailstorms, famines, floods, and generations of animals that lived—and died—before Adam was even created. To many, the idea that God created a world with animal suffering and death and called it "very good" is simply inconsistent with His character. Young earth creationists point out that an ancient creation implies that the earth was a "rough, tough, grizzly place before Adam sinned. There was death all around, catastrophes, disease, genetic defects, freezing cold, burning heat,"[1] and all sorts of things that do not seem "very good."

Since I dug the hole I decided to jump in and asked, "Why do you think an old earth is contrary to God's nature?"

Dr. McLynn fired back, "Because God would not create a world with suffering and call it 'very good.' Adam did not walk on a pile of bones! God brought in death with the curse as a penalty for sin." This seemed to animate her, so she continued, "How could there be death if God called the world 'very good?' In fact, if you allow death before sin, then you destroy the basis for the gospel. Christ died to pay the penalty for sin, but if death existed before sin, death is not a consequence of sin. You throw away the doctrine of atonement if you believe animals died before Adam sinned!" Here was the core of the argument. For Dr. McLynn, suffering and death before the fall nailed the lid shut on the age of the earth debate—it was her theological silver bullet.

More than just accusing old-earth creationists of compromising biblical truth, proponents of the young earth creationism worldview raise the ante and claim that an ancient earth is inconsistent with the gospel. Essentially, what one believes about

---

[1] Van Bebber and Taylor, *"Creation and Time: A Report on the Progressive Creationist Book by Hugh Ross,"* Eden Communications, 1996, p. 18.

animal suffering and death is a litmus test for how genuinely one believes the Bible and even the gospel itself. Because I had dared to consider the possibility of an old earth, I had compromised biblical authority, insulted the character of God, destroyed the basis of the gospel message, and therefore became a heretic.

"Well, I'm not sure that is exactly right," I said. "I certainly don't want to believe something that contradicts the gospel. But still, I think there is more to it. Perhaps Adam is not responsible for all of the suffering in this world. After all, didn't God anticipate that Adam would fall? Of course He did. Otherwise His original plan failed in the garden. What if God had a bigger purpose for creating this world than merely preventing suffering? What if He had a 'Master Plan' to deal with sin and rebellion once and for all eternity, and then take us to an eternal home that really is 'very good?'"

After the word spread of Dr. McLynn's comments to the Women's assembly, our pastor suggested that we should delve a little more deeply to see if we could reach a peaceful resolution. At our pastor's request, two senior associate pastors, the chairman of the deacons, a respected teacher, my friend, and I met weekly for a couple of months to discuss the age of the earth and its relevance to the church. The substance of those meetings culminated with this book.

A Progressing Creationist

Growing up the son of a deacon in a Southern Baptist church, I had always been taught to esteem the Holy Scriptures with the utmost reverence. My teeth were cut on the great doctrines of biblical inspiration and inerrancy. This has not changed. I steadfastly believe that every word of Scripture was breathed by the Holy Spirit, full of meaning and purpose. I believe that God's Word abides forever even though the grass withers and the flowers fade. I believe that heaven and earth will pass away before any jot or tittle of God's Holy Word will pass away.

But I was also a science junky. I was the only kid on our varsity football team who wrote a term paper on Einstein's theory of special relativity. And the more I came to see the majesty of God and His craftsmanship displayed in the heavens, the more I became perplexed about the six days of creation.

Science has built a compelling case that the universe is indeed very old. Science makes it evident that God progressively and miraculously created the universe, prepared the earth for life, and systematically spoke life into existence exactly as described in Genesis—but not in the time frame demanded by the creationist leaders that I had ardently followed. It did not make sense that such great order and design in the heavens and the earth had arisen naturally or that the complexity of life could ever arise apart from divine fiat. But neither did it make sense that every field of science could independently arrive at the same supposedly wrong answer regarding when God created the heavens and the earth.

So I continued to read all the books and attend the young earth creationism seminars. I enthusiastically taught the young earth perspective at youth camps and in Sunday school. But my brain cramp continued to grow—until I came to understand the rest of the story. I still had much more to learn about the theology and science of creation. My progression from a young earth creationist to an old-earth progressive creationist had begun.

Compromise in the Camp

My story is actually quite typical. In evangelical churches around the world Christians are taught that the earth is young because the Bible says so. The message is consistent and clear: what one thinks about the age of the earth is a litmus test for how they regard the Bible and its Author. To even give thought to the notion that the earth is older than ten thousand years is to show disrespect for the authority of Scripture, insult the character of God, and undercut the gospel message.

Young earth creationism leaders describe those who disagree with their view of a recent creation as compromisers. They claim that the compromise is motivated by a desire to find a middle ground in a misguided effort to convert atheistic evolutionists to a more palatable creation story. But that simply is not the case. An unwavering commitment to biblical authority, inerrancy, and the historical accuracy of the Genesis creation account simply does not require belief in six calendar days of creation a few thousand years ago. Far from compromise, an unwaverable pursuit of truth is paramount in our endeavors to see God's hand both in the infallible Scriptures and in His creation.

It is also important to clarify that belief in long ages of creation is not the same as belief in the general theory of evolution. Confusion sometimes results when phrases such as "evolutionary time scales" are used to describe the old earth time-frame. This unfortunate wording blurs the significant distinction between the when and the how of creation. Guilt by association results when evolution is wrongly associated with old earth creationists who accept the overwhelming consensus of scientific evidence for an ancient creation of the earth, but do not hold to the general theory of evolution.[2] To be precise, progressive creationists believe that God miraculously and progressively created life as described in the first chapter of Genesis through long ages of time. Progressive

---

[2] The best resource is the electronic book *Evidences That Have Led Many Scientists to Accept An Ancient Date for Creation of the Earth and Universe*, by Hill Roberts (1998), available online from http://lordibelieve.org. See also Davis Young, *Christianity and the Age of the Earth*, Zondervan, 1982, and G. Brent Dalrymple, *The Age of the Earth*, Stanford University Press, 1991.

creationists do not believe that "time, chance, struggle, and death brought man and other animals into existence."[3] We believe it was the creative power of God that spoke the "kinds" into existence at providentially determined times.

The Larger Issue

More than the age of the earth separates young earth from old earth creationists. In fact, the two camps are built on two very different theological frameworks. Essentially, the difference boils down to two small words: "very good." What did the Creator mean when He pronounced His creation "very good?"

In Sunday school classrooms and pulpits of evangelical churches today, the young earth worldview is the de facto standard. Young earth creationist leaders have asserted themselves as the indefatigable defenders of faith and biblical authority.[4] "As never before we are in the midst of an historic attack on biblical orthodoxy," argues a prominent leader of the young earth creation movement. What is the attack? It is old earth creationism, "a compromising theory which goes to the heart of Christian orthodoxy." An issue that seems arcane at worst to most Christians—animal death before Adam—is trumpeted as "the defining issue for this generation." Why is this issue so important? Because "to believe

---

[3] Morris, Henry III, *After Eden*, Master Books, 2003, p. 189.

[4] It bears pointing out that many evangelical leaders do not concur with the young earth creation view. Notable theologians, pastors, and Christian leaders open to an old earth position include Gleason Archer, Henry Blocher, James Montgomery Boice, William Jennings Bryan, Chuck Colson, Millard Ericksen, Norman Geisler, Jack Hayford, Charles Hodge, Walter Kaiser, C.S. Lewis, J.I. Packer, Pat Robertson, John Sailhamer, Francis Schaeffer, C.I. Scofield, Bruce Waltke, and Benjamin Warfield to name a few.

in death before Adam is to attack the core of biblical orthodoxy on the question of the atonement of Jesus Christ."[5] The idea that there was no animal death before the fall is an emotionally charged, multifaceted issue that is the center of gravity for young earth creationism. On the theological side is the sentiment that an ancient earth is inconsistent with God's character. He simply would not consider a world where animals suffered and died to be "very good." On the philosophical side, the issue of animal immortality is an answer to the problem of suffering if all pain and death originated in man's rebelliousness. And on the scientific side, the concept of original animal immortality is a revered biblical trump card in the game of origins. Essentially the Bible disproves Darwinian evolution if there was no animal death before the sin of man. Thus animal immortality is central to the theology and science of young earth creationism.

Because young earth creationism is ubiquitous in evangelical churches today, an orthodox, biblically based response from an old earth perspective is sorely needed. Committed to the pursuit of truth and the principle of biblical inerrancy, we will consider the theological foundations of young and old earth creation to determine which most accurately represents the nature of God and His revealed plan. This book has three objectives. First, it will show that an ancient creation is utterly faithful to the historical foundations of orthodox evangelical theology. It will present an old earth creation worldview that does not compromise biblical authority, the doctrine of inerrancy, or the character of God. Second, it will examine the theological and scientific aspects of the young earth creation worldview. And third, it will examine "the defining issue for this generation" to uncover what the Bible really teaches about animals before the fall of man.

---

[5] These quotes are from the concluding session (episode 8) of the "After Eden" tape series, a panel discussion from The Institute for Creation Research, 2004.

A few words of caution are in order at this point. First it is very important for readers to understand that the focus is not young earth creation*ists*—it is young earth creation*ism*. This book is not intended to be divisive nor disparaging to fellow believers. In fact, many fellow believers who hold to a recent creation will not agree with every facet of the young earth creationism worldview. Many will read this book and say, "I don't believe that!" But because that worldview forms the context from which much of what is taught in our churches is derived, a critical evaluation of that worldview is long overdue.

It is also important to understand that what is under consideration in this book is a theological framework and not the integrity or sincerity of the people who advocate it. Although we do not agree on some important issues, we wish to disagree with a gentle spirit. By addressing these important but nonetheless contentious topics in creation theology, we hope to bring unity rather than division in the church. Disagreements such as this provide an excellent opportunity to learn if we approach it with humility, a love for each other, and a love for the truth. My sincerest hope is that this book will be used by God to bring insight and understanding regarding the creation paradigms for those who seek His truth.

THINKING BELIEVERS

Her granddaughter simply said, "It was her time." Quite an understatement—Maud Farris-Luse died March 18, 2002, at the ripe old age of 114 years, the oldest living person at that time according to the Guinness Book of World Records. She outlived two husbands and six of her seven children, leaving a legacy of 26 grandchildren, 85 great-grandchildren, 65 great-great-grandchildren, and one great-great-great-grandchild. The same year Mrs. Farris was born, Thomas Alva Edison applied for patents for the phonograph and the telegraph. Both the paper clip and the typewriter ribbon were patented in the year of her birth. Her life spanned the invention of the telegraph and the Internet, the phonograph and the DVD. She witnessed the progression from horse and buggy, to the Wright Brothers' flight, to Charles Lindbergh crossing the Atlantic, to Neil Armstrong stepping onto the surface of the moon, and to men and women living in space. Never before in the history of the world have two eyes witnessed more advancement in knowledge and technology.

But with these advancements has come great arrogance: God has been left behind. Many in our society now claim that, "there is no need of, or use for, a god."[1] Some see the Bible as an irrelevant book of myths. Christianity is dismissed as a relic of a less enlightened time standing in sharp contrast with modern thought and established scientific fact. Even for those who believe in the Creator, exactly how to relate science and faith is not an easy question.

Worldviews Collide

The stakes of this battle are indeed high. Remove God from science and what remains is a materialistic naturalism where life has no transcendent meaning. This godless philosophy of naturalism says:

> We are here because one odd group of fish had a peculiar fin anatomy that could transform into legs for terrestrial creatures; because comets struck the earth and wiped out dinosaurs, thereby giving mammals a chance not otherwise available (so thank your lucky stars in a literal sense); because the earth never froze entirely during the ice age; because a small and tenuous species, arising in Africa a quarter of a million years ago, has managed, so far, to survive by hook and by crook. We may yearn for a 'higher' answer—but none exists.[2]

Scientists are not the only ones who draw lines in the sand. Christians are tempted to disregard science because of the zeal with which some scientists oppose Christian faith. While a scientist may presume Christianity to be irrelevant, a Christian may see science as an enemy of faith. In either case, a great opportunity for seeking truth is lost. It is not necessary for science to exist without God, nor is it wise for the Christian faith to neglect

---

[1] The American Atheist Association.

[2] Gould, Stephen Jay as quoted in David Friend, *The Meaning of Life,* 1991, p. 33.

14

scientific knowledge. There is in fact a higher answer that both science and Christian faith can illuminate.

The battle lines are often drawn between science and the Bible as if the two occupy mutually exclusive domains.[3] Each domain speaks its own language of its own constitution, one spiritual and one material. Essentially, this is Gnosticism dressed in modern clothes. A question submitted to an advice column of a popular magazine illustrates this perspective. The reader asked: "I am a Christian with a firm belief in God; I also believe in dinosaurs. But the Bible says that God created the universe and everything in it, including humans, in seven days. That leaves no time for dinosaurs to roam the Earth for 150 million years. Do you think that believing in dinosaurs makes me any less of a Christian?"

The columnist responded:

Not in my opinion. It's not hard to hold conflicting beliefs if one of them comes from the heart—like religion—and the other comes from the head—like science. In other words, I'm sure you'll never believe in conflicting religions. (You won't be both a Christian and a Muslim.) Likewise, I'm sure you'll never believe in conflicting scientific concepts. (You won't believe both that the earth is round and that it is flat.) That's because I think science arises from the intellect, and religion arises from emotion. I call these beliefs from the heart "emotional logic." Here's an example: Can you imagine falling in love with someone for no reason at all? Of course you can!

---

[3] Stephen Jay Gould developed the theme that science and religion occupy two mutually exclusive domains referred to as "Non-Overlapping Magesteriums" in his book *Rocks of Ages*, published by Ballentine Books, 2002.

Religious belief is defined by this worldview as something distinct from intellectual belief, something that you can hold for "no reason at all." As such, it is completely reasonable for one to hold conflicting views because the two types of belief arise from mutually exclusive domains—the intellect and the emotion, the heart and the head. Conflicting beliefs can peacefully coexist only because they assume that a religious belief system is not based on objective truth or open to rational investigation.

The Bible offers a different perspective. Christianity claims to be true—not true only in some experiential sense, but substantively true in an objective, rational sense. In fact according to Jesus the greatest commandment is to "Love the Lord your God with all your heart and with all your soul and with all your mind" (Matthew 22:37). Thus as Christians we have a divine mandate to apply our minds to our faith as we test our doctrines and seek the truth that God has revealed to us.

The Twenty-First Century Apologist

Modern life does not lend itself to deep thought and investigation. We consume the day's news in seven-second sound bites. Fast paced lifestyles and competing demands for our time do not allow for deep introspection. We don't have the time or energy for critical analysis of difficult issues. Quick answers to difficult questions often have to suffice. But if we are to honor God, we must be thinking believers. This is certainly the case when it comes to the theology and science of creation.

If the church is to engage the marketplace of ideas in the twenty-first century, we must understand the times. Many skeptics and seekers alike see the Christian worldview as anti-intellectual and incompatible with modern life. Some think that Christianity has failed to give a compelling defense for the goodness and power of God in light of the suffering and evil in the world. It is essential that Christians learn to think critically about the difficult issues of the Christian faith. This is certainly the case when it comes to the theology and science of creation.

A Ready Defense

Seekers always ask questions of the Christian faith that believers must be prepared to answer. These questions often challenge the validity of our belief system. The beauty of Christianity, however, is that it is defensible. In fact, we are commanded to defend our faith. Peter challenges believers to be ready to answer such questions: "But sanctify Christ as Lord in your hearts, always being ready to make a defense to everyone who asks you to give an account for the hope that is in you, yet with gentleness and reverence" (1 Peter 3:15).

The defense of our faith goes beyond *what* we believe to giving a reason for *why* we believe. We don't have to answer every question that could possibly be asked, but we must be ready to explain the basis for our beliefs. If our beliefs are unfounded, there is no compelling reason for anyone to share them. Because life and death are held in the balance according to our beliefs, we must be able to explain them to those who do not share our faith.

In addition to positive arguments for the Christian faith and rebuttals of criticisms against the Christian faith, we also must be prepared to expose the weakness in competing worldviews. When a person rejects the truth about God that has been revealed to them, they become "futile in their speculations" (Romans 1:21). We must enter into a spiritual battle for the mind and soul and attack these futile speculations. "For though we walk in the flesh, we do not war according to the flesh, for the weapons of our warfare are not of the flesh, but divinely powerful for the destruction of fortresses. We are destroying speculations and every lofty thing raised up against the knowledge of God, and we are taking every thought captive to the obedience of Christ" (2 Corinthians 10:3–5).

To bring people to a saving knowledge of Christ, we must first remove the roadblocks in their path. At every turn, apologists must be gracious as they tear down the lofty things raised up against the knowledge of God. While the argument might be won, the soul might be lost because of an attitude that fails to demonstrate Christ's love. The Christian spirit is as important as its substance.

A Testable Faith

Far from shying away from the difficult issues and discouraging critical analysis, the Bible invites investigation: "Test everything. Hold on to the good" (1 Thessalonians 5:21 NIV).

While the believer has the inner witness of the Holy Spirit guiding us to all truth, how else are we to compel unbelievers to believe that the Bible is true? Why should someone believe that the Bible rather than the *Qur'an* or *Bhagavad Gita* is the Word of God? We may distinguish between the many world religions only because the Christian faith is verifiable. Likewise, we can only compel the seeker to share our faith if our beliefs are testable and true. The key to being grounded in sound doctrine, not subject to winds or waves of doctrinal change, is to critically evaluate what we believe and stand firmly rooted in the solid foundation of biblical truth. A confident faith results when we examine and test our faith.

A True Faith

Finally, the Christian faith is defensible and testable for the simple reason that it is true. If judgment begins with the people of God (1 Peter 4:17), then we must be willing to put our doctrines to the test. We must never let ideology or our reputation keep us from being committed to a pursuit of the truth. When our interpretations fail to be consistent with God's revealed truth, we must realign ourselves with the truth and return to our testing. If we choose to advance an ideology that does not faithfully adhere to truth, then we have departed from the company of Christ. This sober reality applies equally well to both creation worldviews— indeed it applies to all believers. Let us pray for the grace of God to be humble and courageous in our pursuit of God's unchanging truth; it will stand the test.

Some things we have been taught will not.

CREATION PARADIGMS

The eleventh chapter of the epistle to the Hebrews is perhaps one of the most endearing chapters in the entire Bible, for in this chapter God unveils a "hall of fame" for the great men and women of faith throughout history. Through the eyes of faith, these saints lived with a view toward a sure but unseen day of promise. Each of these saints saw the coming fulfillment of God's eternal plan through the eyes of faith. Each sought a heavenly kingdom, one that God was preparing for them according to His eternal purpose. Not the least of these was the patriarch of God's people, Abraham, who obeyed God by leaving his home and embarking on a journey toward an unknown destination. On his journey he was always looking beyond the next place to pitch his tent, "for he was looking for a city which has foundations, whose architect and builder is God" (Hebrews 11:10).

The eleventh chapter of Hebrews concludes by summarizing the spectrum of trials and tribulations these Old Testament saints endured "in order that they might obtain a better resurrection" (Hebrews 11:35). They understood that their difficulties in this world were part of the cost of participating in God's unfolding plan for human history. Headed for a sure and appointed completion, God's plan included them and their sufferings.

Jesus also taught that His followers would have to count the cost of following Him. God's plan for the righteous is not a path without suffering. Saints throughout history have understood that God allows and even brings difficulties into their lives for a brief time in order to accomplish His eternal purpose. By faith, the saints of old saw the reality of God's hand of providence working in their lives to bring about His predetermined end. They understood that "momentary, light affliction [was] producing . . . an eternal weight of glory" (2 Corinthians 4:17).

Like the saints of old, by faith we must seek to understand the eternal purpose of an all-wise, all-loving, and all-powerful Creator who chose to permit suffering and evil for a time in order to accomplish a greater, eternal good. Our paradigms must allow room for God to be sovereign in the planning and execution of His chosen means to accomplish His eternal purpose.

A Tale of Two Paradigms

A paradigm is like a puzzle where all the pieces fit together to form a view of our world. The various aspects of life fit together to form a (hopefully) consistent picture. Like looking through rose-colored glasses, we see life filtered through our paradigms. But when we try to fit the pieces of daily life into our puzzle, sometimes things just do not seem to fit. Like high school students in a chemistry lab, we often try to explain away what does not fit or else we simply ignore it like bad data.

Science employs paradigms by observing natural events and formulating descriptive models. Competing paradigms are developed as scientists attempt to integrate observations and data in a consistent and coherent manner. Scientific models are constantly under scrutiny to determine which models best fit the available data. As more observations and better data accumulate, paradigms are tested to determine if their perspectives concur with the data. Science progresses as paradigms are either refined or rejected.

Isaac Newton's quest to describe the motion of falling apples and cannon balls is an excellent illustration of paradigms in the progress of science. Newton's laws of gravity dominated science for over two centuries, but his paradigm eventually fell short. A more complete paradigm came two and a half centuries later when Einstein developed his theory of general relativity. Einstein's paradigm superseded Newton's in a way that fundamentally changed the way we view our world.

Theology also employs paradigms to integrate God's revealed truth in a coherent and systematic manner. Hodge refers to theology as "the science of the facts of divine revelation."[1] Just as scientific paradigms are subjected to rigorous analysis based on the available data, theological paradigms must also be tested against the revelation of God to determine the best fit. Like scientific theories, some theological models are refined, some are rejected, and some are inconclusive until we study and learn more.[2]

It is very important to recognize the distinction between paradigms and truth. Paradigms are human constructs—models that attempt to integrate distinct points of fact (the "data" of revelation) into a consistent system from which we can make sense of our world. But as a human construct, a paradigm is fallible and incomplete, even when based on the infallible and complete truth of revelation. This subtle distinction is highly significant when it comes to analyzing our worldviews. Often what someone asserts as the clear reading of Scripture is actually an implication from a particular paradigm. So while the truth of God's word is not in

---

[1] Hodge, Charles, *Systematic Theology*, Vol. I, Wm. B. Eerdmans Publishing Co., 1871, Reprinted May 1993, p. 21.

[2] Even though it is based on the truths of God's inerrant and finished Word, theology is an imperfect science. Often there are multiple theological paradigms available to explain a common set of biblical data. The church has struggled for centuries to bring the facts of biblical revelation into systematic order on doctrines such as predestination and free will or the time of the rapture.

question, His word demands that we test our paradigms to see if they are consistent with His revealed truth.

Paradigms are one part help and one part hindrance when it comes to integrating our finite understanding of the Infinite Creator and the infallible truth of His word. Each of us has a mental picture of what God is like built from what we learn in church, Bible study, and our environment (family, friends, popular culture, etc.). Expecting God to conduct Himself in a certain manner, we interpret life through the perspective of our paradigm. Many crises of faith come about when daily experience or the revelation of God does not fit our paradigm.

But when it comes to the rich doctrines of the Christian faith, we simply cannot ignore the pieces that do not fit our paradigm. A consistent Christian worldview requires us to integrate the doctrines of creation, redemption, and resurrection into a consistent theological system. Spiritual maturity comes as we refine that system to align it with God's revealed truth.

Perhaps nowhere is the significance of the distinction between paradigms and truth more relevant than the topic of creation paradigms. In the chapters to come, we will introduce an old earth creation worldview and examine its biblical basis. We will also examine the biblical basis and scientific aspects of the mainstream young earth creation worldview. These two worldviews will be put to the test to determine which is best aligned with divine revelation and orthodox theology.

The Perfect Paradise Paradigm Defined

Distilled to its essence, the young earth creationism worldview is founded on two words: "very good." At the core of this paradigm is an answer to the question: "When God declared His finished creation 'very good,' what did He mean?" The presumptive meaning of these two words sets the context for every element of the young earth creation worldview.

This idyllic concept of the original creation, which we call the "Perfect Paradise Paradigm," is the theological foundation of young earth creationism.

> Our pure, holy, loving Creator created a paradise for us, designed for our enjoyment. Man had every opportunity to enjoy that perfect world forever. Instead, Adam and Eve rebelled. This sin corrupted their souls and bodies and all paradise—cutting them off from close communion with their holy Creator. Our loving and just God did not choose to destroy them forever. Instead, He immediately set into motion a plan of sacrificial redemption. He provided death, both as a judgment and a blessing, a means of ultimately restoring man to Himself. As a natural result and as a judgment of Adam's sin, death and suffering came upon all the world man ruled and upon all of Adam's descendants. The suffering we experience is the result of human sin; this is not the way God originally wanted things to be. When the perfect time was come, God sacrificed His Son to redeem man and conquer death forever. Ultimately he will restore paradise! Again there will be no death, no suffering, no evil.[3]

There are five basic tenets to this young earth creation paradigm:

1. When God declared His finished creation "very good," He meant that it was perfect in every conceivable way.

2. Eden was the embodiment of the Creator's ideal intent for His creation.

3. Man's sin thwarted God's plan, shattered His ideal intent, and ruined all of His perfect creation.

4. God introduced the physical death of man and animals as a punishment for sin.

---

[3] Van Bebber and Taylor, p. 43–44.

5. God instituted the plan of redemption to reverse the effect of Adam's sin and restore all things back to their original ideal intent.

Most people familiar with creation theology will easily recognize the details of this paradigm. Many will also recognize that these tenets are the de facto perspective on creation taught in evangelical churches. In the chapters to come, we will investigate these five tenets to determine how closely they align with God's revealed truth.

The Perfect Purpose Paradigm Defined

The other paradigm, which we will call the "Perfect Purpose Paradigm," begins by considering the historical roots of orthodox evangelical theology. This paradigm asserts that the world was "very good" from the beginning in light of a specific end. Like the saints in Hebrews eleven, old earth creationists recognize that the Creator's purpose for creation is larger than this life alone. Before time began, the Architect and Builder was looking toward to an eternal city (Hebrews 11:10). That final state (the "better resurrection" in Hebrews 11:35) was already in His mind when He spoke the heavens and the earth into existence. It was very good because it was perfectly suited for the Creator's eternal purpose.

The ultimate end for which this world was created is to glorify the Sovereign Creator. In eternity past, God formulated a 'Master Plan' to accomplish this eternal purpose. His eternal, unchangeable plan called for creation of the spirit realm and anticipated Satan's rebellion against His authority as Sovereign Ruler. The plan of God also called for the creation of the material realm as the stage on which He would judge the adversary and consummate His glorious kingdom. The manifold wisdom of the Master's plan was to glorify Himself through conquering the kingdom of darkness and providing redemption to His beloved image-bearers in one righteous act. After subjecting all authority under the feet of Jesus, the kingdom will be handed over to the Father, who will be all in all. All opposition will have been justly conquered, and evil will have been put away forever. Seeing the infinite wisdom and matchless perfection of God's plan, His redeemed creatures will fully—and freely—serve and glorify Him forever. God Himself will dwell with us, and we with Him. All of history unfolds according to the Master's plan for creation to accomplish His eternal purpose of bringing glory to Himself.

The key to this perspective is to recognize that God had a higher purpose than merely to fellowship with man in a pristine and blissful garden paradise. Rather than the egocentric perspective that God's purpose was our enjoyment, the more cosmic scope of this paradigm properly focuses on the ultimate end of creation which is the glory of God. This eternal perspective accounts for the fuller meaning of the cross where Christ dealt not only with the sin of man but also with the rebellion of Satan. In the economy of the Creator's eternal plan, what began before time will end with the consummation of His kingdom and the demonstration of His glory to all creation for all eternity. It is this biblical truth that establishes the context for an ancient creation worldview.

Man's Thoughts and Ways

At its core, the Perfect Paradise Paradigm envisions an original creation of pristine perfection with no suffering or travail. It was sheer perfection because its perfect Creator called it "very good." It was the absolute very best He could do for us. There could have been no suffering or death in that world. Speaking about an ancient creation, Henry Morris says, "it *seems unthinkable* that the God of the Bible—the God who is omniscient and omnipotent, merciful and loving—would do anything like that. Surely He could devise and implement a *better plan* than this."[4]

Here we see the significance of the distinction between the truth of God's word and our paradigms. Much of the heat in the debate on the age of the earth is due to the sentimental notion of what we think the Creator would consider "very good." For proponents of the Perfect Paradise Paradigm, what seems "very good" becomes the litmus test for determining the correct creation worldview. But God is not bounded by what is thinkable to His creatures. When God does not act in the way we think He should, it reflects the deficiencies of our understanding of God rather than flaws in His true nature. Instead of constraining God to act in a way that appeals to our way of thinking, we must allow for God to act in ways that are befitting a transcendent Creator with an eternal plan.

Higher Thoughts and Ways

It really should come as no surprise that the Creator's plans and actions are often beyond our grasp. The biblical doctrine of creation asserts that the Creator transcends His creation. To be transcendent means that God's nature exceeds the bounds of human capacity. The prophet Isaiah understood this perspective when the LORD spoke through him:

"For My thoughts are not your thoughts,
    Nor are your ways My ways," declares the LORD.
"For as the heavens are higher than the earth,
    So are My ways higher than your ways
    And My thoughts than your thoughts." (Isaiah 55:8–9)

---

[4] Henry Morris, "The Fall, The Curse, and Evolution," Back To Genesis No. 112a, The Institute for Creation Research, April 1998.

The Creator's full glory lies beyond the grasp of the finite mind. His ways are infinitely higher than our ways and His thoughts are immeasurably greater than our thoughts. God is not like a fruit fly that we can examine under a microscope. He is not sitting on the witness stand to be cross-examined by those who do not agree with the way He governs the affairs of His creation. We can only know about God through the things He chooses to reveal to us.

There is much that we can learn about God's purposes and ways of creation from Job and his suffering. Although Job was perfect in God's estimation, he still had a lot to learn about God.[5] This is masterfully demonstrated at the close of the book of Job. After listening to Job defend his own righteousness and question God's justice, God breaks the silence: "Then the LORD answered Job out of the whirlwind and said, 'Who is this that darkens counsel by words without knowledge?'" (Job 38:1–2).

God then proceeds to question Job about the mysteries of His creation and the wisdom of His ways. As example after example is brought to his attention, Job comes to understand the Creator's sovereignty and the transcendent mystery of His ways in the affairs of creation. After the lecture is over, Job humbly acknowledges his limited understanding of God's ways.

Then Job answered the LORD and said,

"I know that You can do all things,
And that no purpose of Yours can be thwarted.
'Who is this that hides counsel without knowledge?'
"Therefore I have declared that which I did not
     understand,
Things too wonderful for me, which I did not know."
(Job 42:1–3)

---

[5] Job gives another perspective on what God considers perfect. He was perfect, but certainly not flawless.

While Job was incapable of understanding all of God's ways, he was not completely wrong. His worldview was vindicated when God rebuked his companions and instructed Job to pray for their forgiveness (Job 42:7–9). Job's friends erred when they relentlessly tried to persuade him about what God would or would not do. Their dogmatic assertions were wrong because their paradigm was wrong. Young earth creationists—indeed all Christians—should heed this warning when they speak definitively about how God must conduct Himself.

When the unavoidable difficult theological issues or the seemingly inconsistent experiences of life run head-long into our Christian worldview, we must be like Job and humbly recognize that our paradigm may be flawed. As if God were telling him to try on the robes of justice, Job is told to ponder the creation if he doesn't like the way God deals with the problem of suffering. Far above ideology or closely held beliefs that are taught with sincere conviction, we must be committed to a ceaseless pursuit of God's revealed truth as we come to know Him and His ways better. With the psalmist, let us pray,

Make me know Your ways, O LORD;

Teach me Your paths.

Lead me in Your truth and teach me. (Psalm 25:4)

The Mystery of His Will

When pondering the mystery of God's ways and the wonder of His nature, we must exercise humility above all else. We should not expect to understand everything about God or the way He conducts Himself in the affairs of men. There will always be things that we do not understand because our knowledge is limited. As Paul wrote, "For now we see through a glass, darkly; but then face to face: now I know in part; but then shall I know even as also I am known" (1 Corinthians 13:12).

We only see part of the story now. The rest will not be clear until we stand in His presence. But rest assured, God has revealed to us exactly what He wants us to know. God has given us everything pertaining to life and to godliness, including "true knowledge of Him" so that we can begin to understand His ways and His plans (2 Peter 1:2). Through His Son, His written word, and His creation, God has given us a wealth of revelation sufficient to occupy us until He returns. Eternity will be insufficient for us to plumb the depths of God's glory and His ways.

Far beyond the scope of human discovery are the unsearchable judgments and unfathomable ways of the transcendent Creator (Romans 11:33). By His grace He chooses to reveal what is hidden behind His impenetrable glory. "Secret things belong unto the Lord our God, but those things which are revealed belong unto us and to our children forever" (Deuteronomy 29:29).

God has given deep truths for us to know and investigate, but, in the words of John Calvin, we must "keep our minds humble." Our paradigms must allow God to work in ways that are counter to our notions of how He should govern the world. Calvin rightly observed that since "God claims to himself the right of governing the world, a right unknown to us, let it be our law of modesty and soberness to acquiesce in his supreme authority regarding his will as our only rule of justice, and the most perfect cause of all things."[6] Spurgeon went so far as to say "we sin in requiring that we should understand God."[7]

This is not an excuse for ignorance or false doctrine: we are held accountable for what we believe. Teachers are held to an even higher standard. We are to search diligently for the truth, test all things, be solidly rooted in sound doctrine, and reject false teaching. Although our knowledge is limited, God only approves of those who rightly divide the truth they have been given (2 Timothy 2:15).

---

[6] John Calvin, *Institutes of the Christian Religion*, Book 1, Chapter 17.

[7] C. H. Spurgeon, "Patient Job, and the Baffled Enemy," in *The Suffering of Man and the Sovereignty of God*, Fox River Press, 2001, p. 52.

Perhaps because He so highly values faith in His followers, or perhaps in order to wage a covert spiritual battle against the enemy, or for reasons not fully known, God chooses to preserve the "mystery of His will" and His ways. That God's ways are often veiled to us or contrary to our preconceived paradigms is the signature of divine authorship. "It is the glory of God to conceal a matter, but the glory of kings is to search out a matter" (Proverbs 25:2). As pointed out by the prophet Isaiah, "Truly, You are a God who hides Himself, O God of Israel, Savior!" (Isaiah 45:15).

It is by design that we are to search out the ways of God and examine His revelation in order to discover His truth. This process of growth and discovery will inevitably challenge our paradigms and push us closer toward truth.

Focal Points

Many have wryly commented, "If I were God, I would do things differently!" Truly, God routinely does things in ways that are counter to our expectations. This notion is vividly demonstrated by the life and death of Christ. The very gospel itself embodies the wisdom of God, but is foolishness to the world. For instance, when Jesus told His disciples that the time had come for Him to suffer, die, and then rise from the grave, Peter thought he knew better. He told the Savior, "God forbid it, Lord! This shall never happen to You." What Jesus said simply did not fit Peter's paradigm. Jesus responded to Peter in the strongest possible way, saying, "Get behind Me, Satan! You are a stumbling block to Me; for you are not setting your mind on God's interests, but man's" (Matthew 16:22–23). Peter learned the hard way that man's ways were not always God's ways.

Lest we make the same mistake as Peter, we should be cautious when we say that God would or should not act in a particular way. Like Peter, we must humbly allow room for the transcendence of God in our understanding of His ways and His plans.

PART 2
THEOLOGY OF
AN ANCIENT CREATION

THE ETERNAL PURPOSE
FOR CREATION

A world characterized by survival of the fittest seems to be anything but a "very good" world. This reasonable sentiment places a burden on old earth creationists to demonstrate that an ancient world with natural disasters and animal brutality could have been intended by the Creator. Old earth creationists must justify how that world would be considered "very good" in His estimation.

To reconcile an ancient creation with the perfection of God's nature requires a paradigm shift. This paradigm shift begins by recognizing that the statement "very good" is a value judgment. Rather than judging the pristine state of that world, a broader perspective suggests that the Creator's appraisal of His creation was based on its fitness for its chosen function. The created world was perfectly suited to accomplish the Creator's perfect purpose. It is exactly at this point—why the Creator considered his creation to be "very good"—that the two creation camps reach a fork in the road.

The Decrees of God

If we are to understand how an ancient world could have been "very good" we must first recognize the Creator's intent for His creation. Was His intent fully realized in the absolute perfection of Eden only to be ruined with one bite of forbidden fruit? Or perhaps did the Creator have a more eternal objective in mind? The answer to this question reveals that an ancient creation is most consistent with His nature.

Theologians determine the Creator's intent by way of the "decrees" of God. According to the Westminster Shorter Catechism, "The decrees of God are His eternal purpose, according to the counsel of His will, whereby for His own glory He hath foreordained whatsoever comes to pass." The decrees of God at once establish the biblical basis for the Perfect Purpose Paradigm while demonstrating cracks in the theological foundation of young earth creationism.

A Singular Purpose

Ultimately there is one purpose behind the Master's plan for creation. In John's vision of heaven, he listens to the twenty-four elders around the throne of God singing a song of worship, saying, "Worthy are You, our Lord and our God, to receive glory and honor and power; for You created all things, and because of Your will (or "pleasure" in the KJV) they existed, and were created" (Revelation 4:11).

The world was created for more than our enjoyment.[1] All things were created expressly for the purpose of the Creator. His "will" is to bring Himself "pleasure" by accomplishing His ultimate purpose for creation. This perspective has been the heart of orthodox evangelical theology since the Reformation. Ultimately, the end for which God created the world is to bring Himself glory.[2]

---

[1] Recall that this is the express reason for the world's creation stated by the young earth creation worldview.

[2] In his essay "The End for Which God Created the World," Jonathan Edwards develops this fundamental truth. He writes, "On the whole, I think it is pretty manifest that Jesus Christ sought the glory of God as his highest and last end, and that therefore . . . this was God's last end in the creation of the world."

God providentially involves Himself in all aspects of His creation to accomplish His ultimate purpose. Thus the Scriptures say, "For from Him and through Him and to Him are all things. To Him be the glory forever" (Romans 11:36). God certainly loves His children, and His plans are for our welfare (John 3:16, Jeremiah 29:11), but His principal aim is His own glory (Isaiah 43:7; 48:9–11).

But what about evil deeds and evil people? In ways that are beyond our understanding, God will ultimately be glorified by all things, even those that are evil: "The LORD hath made all things for himself: yea, even the wicked for the day of evil" (Proverbs 16:4, KJV). Rather than helplessly watching as His creatures thwart His plan, God is actively engaged in all aspects of His creation to accomplish His purpose. God will be glorified in all of His creation. "Whatever He does or permits to be done, is done or permitted for the more perfect revelation of His nature and perfections."[3] This is the purpose for which all things were created. Even the wicked are made for His purpose in His time.

The Bible affirms that the Creator providentially directs the affairs of history "in order that God's purpose according to His choice might stand" (Romans 9:11). A few verses later, Paul describes this interplay between the Creator and His creation: "Or does not the potter have a right over the clay, to make from the same lump one vessel for honorable use and another for common use? What if God, although willing to demonstrate His wrath and to make His power known, endured with much patience vessels of wrath prepared for destruction? And He did so to make known the riches of His glory upon vessels of mercy, which He prepared beforehand for glory" (Romans 9:21–23).

This Scripture emphatically asserts that the Potter has the right to choose the purpose for the vessels. Some vessels are cre-

---

[3] Hodge, Charles, p. 536.

ated for noble purposes, some for common purposes, and some for destruction. Each vessel serves the purpose of glorifying the Potter, either by demonstrating His wrath or making His rich mercy known. Because they were created by Him and for Him according to the Master's plan to bring Himself glory, even vessels of wrath prepared for destruction must ultimately be considered "very good."

Although animal death is less than idyllic, that does not imply that an ancient creation is inconsistent with God's nature. There are many aspects of God's providence that appear less than idyllic from a sentimental perspective. Indeed, that is why we must make room for the transcendent mystery of His ways. Anticipating this objection, Paul clearly states that it is inappropriate for humans to challenge God's eternal purposes (Romans 9:19–20). The clay has no basis for objecting to the sovereign Potter about the finished product. If the Potter can choose the purpose for the clay, the Creator can choose the purpose for His creation. Animal suffering in a temporal world created for His eternal purpose is by no means contrary to His nature.

Some may respond that God permits suffering only in the context of a fallen world. Things are different now because of the sin of man. But did His original purpose only apply before man sinned? Did He originally intend for the world to be pristine with no suffering, only to alter His plans and purpose due to man's sin? Those questions bring us to two more important attributes of God's decrees.

An Eternal Purpose

Not only is the Creator's purpose singular in focus, it is singular in time. The Bible repeatedly refers to the Creator's *eternal* purpose. His eternal purpose predates and motivates His plan for creation. Not only does His eternal purpose address Eden, it encompasses all of human history. The fall of man did not render His purpose irrelevant, a relic to be discarded in favor of another approach. All of history, from Eden to eternity, is unfolding "according to His purpose who works all things after the counsel of His will" (Ephesians 1:11).

The eternal scope of God's purpose establishes the context for the goodness of an ancient creation. Because He is "the beginning and the end" (Revelation 21:6), nothing lies outside the scope of His eternal purpose. Because "His works were finished from the foundation of the world" (Hebrews 4:3), His plan for creation was fixed from beginning to end. Thus more of the creation than Eden was created "very good."

An Unchanging Plan

If the Master's purpose is eternal and His works were finished from the start, then His plan is timeless and unchanging. The immutability of God's plan is grounded in nothing less than the nature of God. Because His plan was formulated in complete knowledge, wisdom, and power there is no need for His plan to be altered. Because His sovereign power brought it to completion, there is no possibility for His plan to be thwarted. The plans of finite men are subject to change because in our limited knowledge and wisdom we cannot foresee the eventual outcome of our actions. Nor do we have at our disposal the power to ensure that our plans will be completed. God, however, is sovereign over all creation and able to fulfill his plan.

Believing that God could allow His plan to be subverted or thwarted in any way against His will, even by evil creatures with evil intentions, would be nothing short of denying the Creator's sovereignty over His creation. A creation that is perfect is one that will achieve the Creator's purpose. As Hodge says, "It is inconsistent with the idea of absolute perfection, that the purposes of God are successive or that He ever purposes what He did not originally intend."[4] To further drive the point home Pink says, "God must

---

[4] Hodge, Charles, p. 537.

either . . . accomplish His will, or be thwarted by His creatures
. . . God is the Creator, and endless ages before man first saw the
light 'the mighty God' (Isaiah 9:6) existed, and ere the world was
founded, made His plans; and being infinite in power and man
only finite, His purpose and plan cannot be withstood or thwarted
by the creatures of His own hands." [5]

Throughout the Scriptures this truth is consistently repeated;
God's plan is unchanging, from beginning to end, and sure to be
accomplished. Through the prophet Isaiah, God declares:

"I am God, and there is no one like Me,

Declaring the end from the beginning,

And from ancient times things which have not been done,

Saying, 'My purpose will be established,

And I will accomplish all My good pleasure' . . .

Truly I have spoken; truly I will bring it to pass.

I have planned it, surely I will do it. (Isaiah 46:9–11)

Again Isaiah states that what God has planned, He will do:
"Even from eternity I am He, and there is none who can deliver out
of My hand; I act and who can reverse it?" (Isaiah 43:13).

An indisputable biblical truth is that when God plans or acts,
no one—neither Satan nor Adam—can reverse it.[6]

---

[5] Pink, Arthur W., *The Sovereignty of God,* Baker Books, 1984, pp. 14–15.

[6] Prophecy provides an interesting proof of the immutability of God's plan.
It is because the eternal plan was formed in advance with full knowledge of
the future and the power to bring it to completion that the future can be told
from the past. If God's plan were subject to change, then the end could not be
declared from the beginning. But because God's eternal plan is immutable,
His "purpose will be established" and He "will accomplish all [His] good
pleasure." It is the certainty ensured by sovereignty that enables predictive
prophecy.

Can it be made more explicitly clear? He declared the end of creation before He began creating; His purpose will not change; He will accomplish what He intends for creation; He will bring His plans to pass.

The Ultimate Good

The ultimate example of God's singular focus on His purpose and His plan to address evil is the sacrificial death of His Son. Jesus became the atoning Sacrifice that satisfied the righteous requirements of God's law and demonstrated God's glory. The Master's plan was "to demonstrate His righteousness, because in the forbearance of God He passed over the sins previously committed; for the demonstration, I say, of His righteousness at the present time, so that He would be just and the justifier of the one who has faith in Jesus" (Romans 3:25–26).

This passage helps us understand how an ancient world could be considered "very good" in light of the Creator's perfect purpose. God patiently "passed over" the sins of humanity from the beginning until the time of Christ because He knew the time of atonement was coming. For a time, the debt piled up without a payment. But God graciously and patiently extended credit in light of the foreordained and pre-planned payment to be made on the cross.

Why did His plan require that He patiently endure unrecompensed evil for a time? Was it because His plan had been thwarted and He was waiting for Plan B to take effect? No, God's original, perfect plan called for this patient forbearance of evil in order to accomplish His intent. The cross was not merely a means to recover what was lost in the garden. The cross was chosen before time began as the means to accomplish His eternal purpose. At the fullness of time He would demonstrate His righteousness to all of His creation. This was the perfect intent in the Master's plan.

At the cross we see a distinct difference between the two creation paradigms. Certainly it was because of His great love for

His image-bearers that the Father sacrificed His Son. Both camps agree that the greatness of Jesus' love for His people was demonstrated on the cross. But it was more than love for His people that held Jesus to the cross. Beyond the nails and beyond the love, His principle aim was for the Father and the Son to be glorified.

As if all of history had been anticipating the very moment of his death, Jesus said, "Father, the hour has come; glorify Your Son, that the Son may glorify You" (John 17:1). History was brought to this point for the realization of the Father's eternal purpose. Jesus prayed to the Father for His children to have eternal life so that they might know Him and glorify Him. His desire for us to be with Him in eternity was not merely to restore the fellowship broken by the fall. Much more, He wants us to be with Him so that we can behold His glory (John 17:24). Jesus obeyed the Father to the point of death and was given a name above all other names so that the Father would be glorified (Philippians 2:8–11). There is no greater demonstration of God's plan involving suffering and death as a means to the end of His purpose than the life and death of Immanuel, God with us.

The Impact of the Fall

The sharpest theological divide between the two creation paradigms deals with how the fall of man affected the Creator's purpose for His creation. The foundational premise of the Perfect Paradise Paradigm is that the original world was "very good" because it was the embodiment of sheer perfection. Young earth creationism asserts that the Creator's intent was fully realized in Eden, only to have that intent thwarted by the rebellion of man. God's plan then took a detour when Adam and Eve ate from the forbidden tree and brought suffering and death into the world. One leader of the young earth creationism movement describes the impact of the fall on God's plans as follows:

In the beginning man enjoyed full fellowship with God,

THE ETERNAL PURPOSE FOR CREATION

but soon rejected Him, bringing the ruination of all creation. This wasn't God's intention, so He implemented His plan for creation to fulfill its intended purpose. . . . Unfortunately, the present world with sin and its penalty permeating all things and processes, temporarily experiences the postponement of His ultimate plan, but it will not be forever thwarted. There will be the "new heavens and a new earth, wherein dwelleth righteousness" (2 Peter 3:13) once again. This is His plan, purpose, and pleasure.[7]

Here we see a clear distinction between the two creation paradigms. Exactly what was the Creator's "plan, purpose, and pleasure?"

According to the Perfect Paradise Paradigm, the chief end of creation was fully realized in Eden. When sin thwarted the original intent of the Creator, the Perfect Paradise ended. Implicit in the Perfect Paradise Paradigm is the belief that God's "ultimate plan" was "thwarted" and "postponed" so that God had to resort to another plan.

While this perspective helps account for unseemly things in this world, it does so by enabling man to thwart the plan of God. Theologians will continue to wrestle with the interplay between God's sovereignty and man's free will, but we must concur with Job when he said to God, "no purpose of Thine can be thwarted" (Job 42:2). Scriptures consistently reveal that God designed all of creation according to His eternal purpose to bring about His predetermined conclusion. God did not finish His work in the garden of Eden and sit back to watch, hoping that man would not ruin His plan. His plan was set in motion in the garden and continued unabated after Eden.

---

[7] Morris, John D., "Why Did God Create Us?" Institute for Creation Research, July 2002.

If one takes the perspective that the Creator's purpose encompassed not only the creation but also the rebellion of Satan, the fall of man, and the entirety of human history, it is evident that the original creation did not have to be unblemished and pristine. Rather, it is in light of that eternal purpose that the world was declared "very good." The goodness of creation and creation's correspondence with the nature of God can only be judged in light of the completion of His plan, not merely its beginning.

Once the Creator's assessment of creation is seen from the perspective of His singular, immutable, eternal purpose, it becomes clear that He had more in mind than Eden alone. His aim was fixed on a greater good than creating and preserving the pristine sanctity of Eden. From eternity past, His purpose had always been to bring Himself glory. Having completed His work of creation, He surveyed all He had done and declared it to be "very good." Now the stage was perfectly set for the unfolding of His perfect plan.

Focal Points

Young earth creationism presumes that God's intended purpose for creation was realized in Eden, but in His foreknowledge He planned a provision for man's fall. Thus the implemented plan was not the original ideal embodied in Eden. Perhaps that is the case. However, that premise seems difficult to reconcile with the biblical truth that there was only one plan to accomplish an eternal purpose and that plan did not change after Eden. God's plans are not merely wishful thinking, but rather the embodiment of His manifold wisdom, empowered by His sovereignty, purposed to bring Him glory and pleasure. To argue that the Creator's plan was thwarted and altered by the sin of man is essentially to deny the sovereignty of God. According to Hodge, "it would reduce

God to the level of His creatures, to assume that what He decrees, should fail to come to pass."[8]

Moreover, if God's plan was thwarted at the fall of man, how could there be any assurance that His new plan would not also fail? If Adam interrupted His ultimate plan, then could not some other creaturely action possibly change God's plan again? The faithfulness of God would be nullified, and His uniqueness as demonstrated by prophecy would be invalidated if the end of His eternal, unchanging plan were not certain. Indeed, God makes it clear that His plan and His work were finished before He began.

Was the Creator's plan for man to dwell in blissful perfection as long as he avoided that lone forbidden tree? Or was it a singular, eternal plan, formulated before time began and played out through time in human history? In the next chapter we will consider the bigger picture to understand what was the Creator's eternal plan and how that plan relates to an ancient creation and animal suffering before the fall.

---

[8] Hodge, Charles, p. 541.

THE DRAMA OF ALL TIME

In the last chapter we observed that the two creation paradigms differ primarily on the Creator's ultimate intent for creation. In this chapter we will probe more deeply into the Creator's plan for accomplishing His intent. More than merely focusing on fellowship with His image-bearers in a perfect world, the Scriptures reveal a more eternal perspective on the Creator's intent, a perspective that views this world as a stage on which the drama of His plan is unfolding through human history.

A Cosmic Crisis

The Bible reveals to us a hostile reality beyond the boundaries of the physical world. Although we "walk in the flesh," history is immersed in the context of a cosmic spiritual battle (2 Corinthians 10:3–5). From the unreachable depths of eternity past, God has reigned supremely, uncontested in His triune sovereignty as "all in all." So how did this conflict arise?

At some unknown point after the Creator punctuated the solitude of His triune glory and created the angelic hosts, a dark cloud of insurrection arose in the Kingdom of Light. Satan, a proud angel, rebelled against his Creator, challenging the Master's Kingdom and bringing about a temporal state of cosmic discord. This rebellion did not surprise the King. Anticipating this fall in the spirit realm, the eternal and immutable plan of God was unfolding to accomplish the Master's purpose. Perhaps God ultimately created the physical world to repair this cosmic breach as the preferred means of bringing glory to Himself.

While the Scriptures do not say exactly when the fall of Satan occurred, some commentators presume that it occurred after the sixth day. According to proponents of the Perfect Paradise Paradigm, God would not consider creation "very good" if part of it—Satan and his angelic companions—had already rebelled. This is a prime example of two small words casting a long shadow. Although we do not know when Eve was tempted, there is no biblical reason to presume that the rebellion of Satan and his expulsion from heaven occurred between the sixth day and Eve's temptation.

The Bible does actually imply that Satan fell before the physical world was created. Jesus indicated that Satan rebelled before creation began when He said that the devil "was a murderer from the beginning" (John 8:44). Likewise, John also tells us "the devil has sinned from the beginning" (1 John 3:8). If the devil sinned from the beginning, then the fall of Satan occurred before the beginning and not some time after creation was declared "very good."

Many theologians have placed the fall of Satan prior to the creation of the material world and associated that first fall with God's motivation for creation.[1] Regardless of the time when Satan

---

[1] The prevailing theological paradigm for reconciling Genesis with science at the turn of the twentieth century was the gap theory. This paradigm wrongly inserted an indeterminately long period of time between the first two verses of Genesis. This "gap" represented a time when God devastated His original creation as part of the judgment against Satan before beginning the six days

fell, two important facts remain. First and foremost, God's unchanging, eternal purpose and plan for creation was fixed before He created the physical realm. Second, the fall of Satan occurred before the fall of Adam. Evil was present in the garden even before the forbidden fruit was eaten. Since it was Satan who first rebelled, Adam cannot be solely culpable for the introduction of all evil and suffering into God's perfect creation. The young earth creationism paradigm tends to neglect the significance of Satan's fall in the economy of God's plan as it relates to the problem of suffering and the Creator's original intent.

An Eternal Perspective

While young earth creationism theology envisions a perfect earthly paradise as the Creator's ultimate intention, the Scriptures consistently present a more eternal perspective. A better view is to enlarge the scope of our vision and recognize that this world was created to demonstrate God's glory by dealing with the rebellion of Satan through the redemption of fallen man.

God created this world with the ultimate purpose of demonstrating His glory at the end of history rather than the beginning. His plan to accomplish that eternal purpose was only beginning to unfold when He declared His creation "very good." To understand how an ancient creation is completely consistent with His ultimate purpose, we need to look beyond Eden and see the rest of the story.

The Perfect Purpose Paradigm is deeply rooted in Paul's great manifesto of Christian hope found in 1 Corinthians 15. Our hope

---

of "recreation." Although it has properly fallen out of favor, the gap theory correctly recognized the role Satan's rebellion played in setting the context for the Master's plan for creation. See for example Donald Grey Barnhouse, *The Invisible War*, Zondervan Publishing House, 1965, and Watchman Nee, *Mystery of Creation*, Christian Fellowship Publishers, Inc., New York, 1981.

derives from the assurance of resurrection that leads to the ultimate cosmic triumph of Christ. "For as in Adam all die, so also in Christ all will be made alive. But each in his own order, Christ the first fruits, after that those who are Christ's at His coming . . ."

What is the order Paul is referring to? It is the systematic unfolding of God's eternal plan through the dimension of time. Here we see God's plan progressing after Eden and connecting Adam to Christ. The Master's plan to accomplish His eternal purpose is spelled out as Paul continues. "Then comes the end, when He hands over the kingdom to the God and Father, when He has abolished all rule and all authority and power. For He must reign until He has put all His enemies under His feet. . . . When all things are subjected to Him, then the Son Himself also will be subjected to the One who subjected all things to Him, so that God may be all in all" (1 Corinthians 15:20–28).

The fall of Adam sets the stage for the death and resurrection of Christ and the drama culminates with the end goal of creation— "that God may be all in all."

History is not being driven by the winds of chance or the deeds of men, but is providentially directed toward the end for which the world was created. Before the foundation of the world God laid out an eternal and immutable plan for the ages that saw through the rebellion of Satan and the fall of Adam to the cross of Christ. Having conquered all opposition, all enemies will be put under His feet and all authority subjected to Him. The eternal plan of God is unfolding through history in a deliberate, systematic fashion, leading to *the end* when Christ will finally hand over his kingdom to the Father who will rule supremely as all in all for eternity.

This eternal perspective pervades the mindset of the Apostle Paul. He again spells it out in the first chapter of Ephesians. The Master's eternal plan was formulated in eternity past when "He chose us in Him before the foundation of the world" (verse 4). The Creator's gaze was not fixed on Eden—His plan was formulated "with a view to an administration suitable to the fullness of the times, that is, the summing up of all things in Christ, things in the heavens and things on the earth" (verse 10). When that administration is realized, Christ will reign above all other dominions for all eternity (verses 20–21). The rebellion of Satan will have been put down when He has "put all things in subjection under His feet" and Christ is "head over all things" (verse 22). The eternal purpose of the Father will not be accomplished until the culmination of His plan at the "fullness of the times."

Before creation began and before the creatures rebelled, the Master's plan was intently focused on a coming "administration" that would rule over all and glorify God. It is with that administration in view that the initial acts of the creation drama were called "very good."

The Cosmic Scope of Atonement

Paul's letter to the Colossians describes Christ as the central figure in the Master's plan for cosmic reconciliation, serving as both the agent of creation and the agent of reconciliation. "For by Him all things were created, both in the heavens and on earth, visible and invisible, whether thrones or dominions or rulers or authorities—all things have been created through Him and for Him . . . so that He Himself will come to have first place in everything. For it was the Father's good pleasure for all the fullness to dwell in Him, and through Him to reconcile all things to Himself . . . whether things on earth or things in heaven" (Colossians 1:16, 18–20).

According to the Master's plan, in Christ the Creator became the Redeemer. Note the cosmic scope of Christ's mission. His work addresses human and spirit realms, as well as the past, present, and future. This pleases the Father for a reason—Christ accomplishes the Father's eternal purpose by coming "to have first place in everything."

All things were created "by Him and for Him," that is, according to His plan and to bring about His purposes. Knowing that Satan would rebel and that Adam would sin, Christ created both in order to achieve His purpose. The Creator did not passively or helplessly watch His plan go awry at the fall. "God is no idle spectator, looking on from a distant world at the happenings on earth, but is Himself shaping everything to the ultimate promotion of His own glory. Even now He is working out His eternal purpose, *not only in spite of human and Satanic opposition, but by means of them*"[2] (emphasis mine). The Creator's plan extends beyond the rebellion of His creation to the ultimate realization of His eternal purpose through His creation.

As we saw in the last chapter, Christ's work of atonement is the key theological distinction between the two creation paradigms. While the young earth creationism worldview sees it as a means of recovery after the Creator's original intent was thwarted, the old earth paradigm sees it as the cornerstone of God's unchanging plan through which His eternal purpose is accomplished. Christ's mission was determined before Satan rebelled, the world was formed, or man had fallen. Ironically, it is through the rebellion of His creation that His glory will be more perfectly manifested.

From our perspective the justification of fallen man is the most important aspect of the plan of redemption, but the Master's plan has a more cosmic scope. Christ's death and resurrection brought about the defeat of Satan and the demonstration of God's glory to all of creation. Taken together, these three aspects of Christ's work unveil the cosmic scope of the Master's plan for creation.

Justified by Grace

To us, the most significant aspect of God's plan is the truth that redemption brings about legal acquittal of guilt for the child

---

[2] Pink, p. 240.

of God before the Supreme, Holy Judge. However, this aspect of redemption is not strictly concerned with its benefit to humanity.[3] Those who are acquitted are first created for His glory (Isaiah 43:7). While being the chosen recipients of God's blessings and joint heirs with Christ, the greater end of our redemption is the glory of the Creator. Theologians have noted that the Master's works of creation and redemption "were not due to the desire for happiness and holiness of the creature. They were, instead, formulated with a view to His own glory—in order to display His glory and in order to receive glory from the creature."[4] Redemption was planned by the Father not merely for our benefit but even more to display His glory.

This truth—that redemption was principally purposed for God's glory—serves to illuminate a subtle but significant theological implication in the young earth creationism paradigm. According to the Perfect Paradise Paradigm, God's ideal intention was realized in Eden. Hence, the Father's ultimate intent was supposedly for man to perpetually have direct access to Him. If Edenic conditions prevailed, then there would be no sin to separate the Holy One from His image-bearers. This implies that it was God's highest preference for there to be no need of or place for a Redeemer. As a consequence, the Perfect Paradise Paradigm implies that the Father's ultimate intent for Christ was solely as Creator and only in recourse as Redeemer. The redemptive work of Christ was "Plan B" if Edenic perfection was "Plan A."

This subtle implication suggests a contradiction between Scripture and the Perfect Paradise Paradigm. The presumption that God's ideal intent was embodied in Eden is incorrect, for Scripture repeatedly and emphatically teaches that the Father's

---

[3] Scripture repeatedly asserts that the goal of redemption is first and foremost the glory of God. In addition to the verses cited above, see John 7:18; 12:23,27–28; 13:31–32; 17:1,4–5; and Ephesians 1:3,12,14.

[4] Thiessen, H. C., *Introductory Lectures in Systematic Theology*, Wm B. Eerdmans Publishing Company, Grand Rapids, MI, 1949, p. 171.

preferred means for man to have access to Him has always and only been through His Son. His plan has always been to adopt us through the work of His beloved Son (Ephesians 1:4–5). Our predestined means of access, the means chosen for us before creation began, has always been "in Him."

The Father's original intent was to bring glory to His Son through His redemptive role, for Christ is "the Lamb slain from the foundation of the world" (Revelation 13:8, KJV). Redemption was His ultimate preferred intent expressly so that Christ "will come to have first place in everything" (Colossians 1:18). For if Edenic conditions had been the preference and His preference were realized, then God's image-bearers would have entered His presence on their own merits. Heaven would hold no honor for the redemptive work of Christ. The church would not be the bride, purchased by the One with a name above all other names. The twenty-four elders would not sing to Christ, "Worthy art Thou . . . for Thou was slain" (Revelation 5:9). The myriads of angels would not loudly declare "Worthy is the Lamb that was slain to receive power and riches and wisdom and might and honor and glory and blessing" (Revelation 5:12). What a different place heaven would be if Edenic conditions were the Father's preference.

God never intended for man to spend eternity in His presence without the enabling intercessory work of Christ. "The redemption of sinners by Christ was no mere afterthought of God: it was no expediency to meet an unlooked-for calamity. . . . From all eternity God designed that our world should be the stage on which He would display His manifold grace and wisdom in the redemption of lost sinners."[5]

This point also serves to illustrate why the Bible instructs us to test all things. In much the same way that scientific theories are tested by the predictions they make, the implications of a creation

---

[5] Pink, p. 111.

54

paradigm must agree with sound doctrine. I am certainly not suggesting that young earth creationists knowingly teach false doctrine. Instead, the internal contradiction between the biblical truth of God's plan of redemption and the supposed paradise of Eden has simply not been critically evaluated and brought to light.

With regard to the test of creation paradigms, if the Creator did not declare His creation "very good" because it was an absolutely pristine, perfect world, then He must have meant something else. If the Creator instead considered His creation to be "very good" because it was the perfect stage for the unfolding of His perfect plan, then there is nothing about an ancient creation that conflicts with His nature or His word. Animal suffering and death before the fall only conflict with the idyllic notion of a pristine sanctity called Eden.

Victory in Jesus

More than only paying the penalty for our sin before a holy and just Judge, the cross was also the means by which Christ conquered Satan. God dealt with his rebellion in an unexpected way—He entered creation as a man and overcame Satan through His own death and resurrection. On the cross, the domain of darkness was overthrown by the kingdom of God (Colossians 1:13–14). This moment in history was the decisive victory in the battle for supremacy in the heavenly realms. Christ's victory gave Him the right to rule over his vanquished foe and rescue the prisoners of war. To the victor go the spoils.

Christ's death and resurrection did more than simply redeem man; much more, it was a deathblow to the rebellious aspirations of Satan. The cross became the means of Satan's defeat. Christ was well aware of this for at the time of his crucifixion he boldly declared: "Now judgment is upon this world; now the ruler of this world will be cast out . . . the ruler of this world has been judged" (John 12:31; 16:11). This oft-overlooked aspect of redemption is quite significant for understanding the Master's plan.

More than just paying our debt, the cross stripped away the power of those who held us captive. The rulers of the kingdom of darkness have now been "dethroned and incapacitated, and the shameful tree has become the victor's triumphant chariot, before which his captives are driven in humiliating procession, the involuntary and impotent confessors of his superior might."[6] On the cross, Christ's sovereign rule over all principalities and powers was affirmed in a public display of His glory. As Paul says, "When He had disarmed the rulers and authorities, He made a public display of them, having triumphed over them through Him" (Colossians 2:15).

Whereas God could have immediately put down the challenge of Satan before time began, He chose instead to defeat Satan on an earthly stage in the fullness of time. In a degree of fairness that rivals the measure of God's majesty, God allowed the kingdom of darkness to engage the kingdom of light for cosmic supremacy. Defeating the enemy through the cross was a manifestly wise, fair, and just means of accomplishing the Master's eternal purpose. This glorious truth lies entirely outside the scope of the Perfect Paradise Paradigm: redemption was the means chosen before the creation and fall of man by which the Father dealt with Satan's rebellion.

The Glory of God in the Ages to Come

The first two aspects of redemption please God by reversing the negative effects of Satan's rebellion and Adam's fall. To understand why God permitted these two acts of rebellion—which lies at the core of the problem of suffering—brings us to the essence of God's purpose for creation. The Master's plan for creation continued unfolding after Eden so that His glory would be made known in the ages to come and in the heavenly realms.

---

[6] Bruce, F.F., *New International Commentary on the New Testament, The Epistles to the Colossians, to Philemon, and to the Ephesians*, Wm. B. Eerdmans Publishing Co., 1984, p. 111.

Rather than the ages past, Paul makes it clear that the object of His intent is the ages to come: "But God, being rich in mercy, because of His great love with which He loved us, even when we were dead in our transgressions, made us alive together with Christ (by grace you have been saved), and raised us up with Him, and seated us with Him in the heavenly places in Christ Jesus, so that in the ages to come He might show the surpassing riches of His grace in kindness toward us in Christ Jesus" (Ephesians 2:4–7).

Looking back to Eden is not the direction of the Creator's gaze; the Master's plan is focused on a future time. Having "a view to an administration suitable to the fullness of times, that is, the summing up of all things in Christ, things in the heavens and things upon the earth" (Ephesians 1:10), the Master's intent is fixed on the ages to come. We are redeemed here and now for a demonstration of God's glory in the future.

Nor was humanity the myopic focus of the Creator's plan. A few verses later in the second chapter of Ephesians, Paul identifies the audience for the demonstration in the ages to come. Here Paul shares an insight into the transcendent mystery of God's eternal plan: that redemption is concerned with more than restoring fellowship with man. It was always intended as a cosmic demonstration of God's glory.

To me, the very least of all saints, this grace was given, to preach to the Gentiles the unfathomable riches of Christ, and to bring to light what is the administration of the mystery which for ages has been hidden in God who created all things; so that the manifold wisdom of God might now be made known through the church to the rulers and the authorities in the heavenly places. This was in accordance with the eternal purpose which He carried out in Christ Jesus our Lord. (Ephesians 3:8–11)

Here we see the manifold wisdom of God's eternal plan unfolding. The Creator's plan vastly exceeds the egocentric ideal of the Creator and the creature walking in a perfect garden paradise. Scripture reveals the cosmic scope of the Creator's eternal plan, a plan that was:

1. A mystery hidden for ages,

2. Intended to make known the manifold wisdom of God,

3. Made known through the church,

4. Made known to the rulers in heavenly places.

5. Consistent with the Creator's eternal purpose,

6. Carried out in Christ.

This is a peek behind the impenetrable veil of God's hidden mystery. The Master's purpose for creation was to demonstrate the glory of His wisdom, not only to humanity, but also to the spiritual rulers and authorities. These rulers and authorities are identified in Ephesians as "the devil" and the "spiritual forces of wickedness in the heavenly places" (6:11–12). Thus the church will serve as a demonstration of God's glory to all of creation throughout eternity.

Clearly the plan transcends the supposed perfection of paradise. When the finished creation was declared "very good," much more was in mind than an idyllic world without suffering or animal death. A majestic truth of Scripture is that God's purpose for creation is much greater than a garden paradise for man's enjoyment.

The Grand Finale

One of the most high-tech and unconventional aircraft in the world today is the F-117 Nighthawk Stealth Fighter. Looking more like a bat than an airplane, its abrupt angles and special coatings make it virtually invisible to radar. It was also one of the most closely guarded military secrets in history, flown only at night under the cloak of darkness. So secret was this project that the military did not even admit it existed for more than twenty years. When its existence was finally acknowledged in 1988, it was revealed that over 50 aircraft had been flying from an ultra-secret test facility in the Nevada desert for seven years.

What if a spy had found a way to see this magnificent aircraft? What words would he use to describe this radical, new, secret weapon that only a few eyes had ever seen? And imagine how much greater that challenge would be if the spy had been brought here by a time machine from three millennia ago. What possible language could he use to describe the awesome sight? A similar yet incomparably greater challenge was given to the prophet Isaiah when he penned his inspired vision of the final acts in the drama of creation.

With that in mind, look at how Isaiah paints a picture of the indescribable messianic kingdom: "'The wolf and the lamb will graze together, and the lion will eat straw like the ox; and dust will be the serpent's food. They will do no evil or harm in all My holy mountain,' says the LORD," (Isaiah 65:25). In further detail he writes the following:

> And the wolf will dwell with the lamb, and the leopard will lie down with the young goat, and the calf and the young lion and the fatling together; and a little boy will lead them. Also the cow and the bear will graze, their young will lie down together, and the lion will eat straw like the ox. The nursing child will play by the hole of the cobra, and the weaned child will put his hand on the viper's den. They will not hurt or destroy in all My holy mountain, for the earth will be full of the knowledge of the LORD as the waters cover the sea. (Isaiah 11:6–9)

The book of Revelation also uses vivid imagery to describe the final phase of the Master's plan foretold by Isaiah (Revelation

21:1–5). This phase is the time that the Creator and the creation have been longing for since the beginning.

Paradise Reclaimed

Fundamental to the Perfect Paradise Paradigm is the notion that God will restore the paradise that was lost when Adam sinned. Interestingly, this idyllic view of Eden is derived more from the biblical description of the end times than the beginning.

Isaiah's use of the wolf and the lamb to describe his vision of things yet unseen is assumed by proponents of young earth creationism to be "a beautiful picture . . . of the divinely intended relationships in God's animal kingdom."[7] Advocates of the Perfect Paradise Paradigm write: "Whether this passage describes conditions on the earth in the coming kingdom age after Christ returns to Earth (as I personally believe) or not, it must at least describe the ideal conditions intended by God for His animal creation. Therefore, this must have been the way it was in the beginning, after God had completed His creation work, and surveyed it with deep satisfaction."[8]

But why must this describe the ideal intended by the Creator? Why must it have been this way in the beginning? For those who hold to this paradigm, the answer is that it must have been this way simply because God called His finished creation "very good."[9] Perhaps here most of all is the weight of those two words fully exerted.

---

[7] Morris, Henry, "The Wolf and the Lamb," BTG No. 69a, September 1994.

[8] Morris, Henry, *The Genesis Flood* and "The Wolf and the Lamb," BTG No. 69a, September 1994.

[9] We will address the diets of animals before the fall in a later chapter.

Apart from a sentimental assumption of what is "very good," an objective look at Isaiah's prophecy of the messianic King and His coming rule shows that he is not describing the Creator's intent for life in Eden.[10] Using language and concepts familiar to his time, Isaiah is describing a very different world that "eye has not seen and ear has not heard." A literal description of a world where a wolf and a lamb share a den and where a rattlesnake replaces a rattle as the toddler toy of choice is not his intent. The familiar imagery of this idyllic scene is "a highly symbolic and poetic description of the complete harmony and peace which is to prevail with the coming of the messianic age."[11]

The language of millennial kingdom prophecy is not always to be taken literally. Young earth creationism literally interprets Isaiah's prophecies (11:7; 65:25) to mean that lions will be vegetarians at the end just as they supposedly were at the beginning. But astute readers will note that in another passage describing the peace and safety of the millennial kingdom, Isaiah says "no lion will be there" (35:9). Sandwiched in between the description of lions grazing in the kingdom, Isaiah says that there will be no lions in the kingdom. If the statements are literal, then there is a clear contradiction. But Isaiah is not concerned with a literal description of God's intent for the animal kingdom. Rather, his point is to paint a picture of serene tranquility, a place of perfect peace.

This picture of a future time when man and beast blissfully live together is not meant to describe life as it was in Eden. In fact, Isaiah's prophecy contradicts the very point made by young earth

---

[10] The paradise motif is common in the Old Testament and other ancient writings. Isaiah 65 speaks of a life-giving tree, a serpent eating dust, blessed labor, and childbirth. The imagery does not demand a literal restoration of Eden as much as connoting a time when sin does not reign.

[11] *The Broadman Bible Commentary*, Broadman Press, Nashville, Tennessee, 1971, p. 232.

creationism regarding animal death before the fall. Life in that age will be long and prosperous, but there will be funerals. Human death is still inevitable in the millennial kingdom (Isaiah 65:20). There will be animal death as well. Isaiah's prophecy simply is not a description of the final restoration of the way things were in Eden.

There are references to the paradise motif in other Old Testament prophecies, but they do not establish the notion of a literal paradise with no animal death that will be one day fully restored. Harkening back to the garden to describe the abundance of the millennial kingdom, Ezekiel says that there will be rivers of fresh water and all kinds of trees for food. These rivers will be so full of fish that all along its banks "there will be a place for the spreading of nets" (47:10:12). So even if there is abundant fruit, there will also be abundant fish to be killed and eaten as well. Millennial kingdom prophecy simply does not establish that animals were immortal before the fall.

Focal Points

Yogi Berra is not a theologian, but he got it right when he said: "The future ain't what it used to be." The Scriptures reveal that the Master's plan culminates with a better future than the past has been. When Jesus spoke of the future Kingdom of God, He referred to it as "the kingdom prepared for you from the foundation of the world" (Matthew 25:34). He did not consider it to be a restoration of a previous perfect state, but a unique kingdom prepared for that time from the beginning. Prior to creation and the fall, the Master was planning this final kingdom, one that will be better than anything we have seen or heard. It is not a restoration of Eden because the eyes of man have already beheld that paradise. The future spoken of by Isaiah is a better paradise than the original "very good" creation.

The plan of God goes beyond redemption simply as a means to restore what was broken by the sin of man and the rebellion of Satan. The eternal purpose behind the Master's plan ultimately boils down to His desire to glorify Himself. Redemption, then, is God's greatest tool for bringing about his desired end. The wisdom of God's purpose was to use the plan of redemption to destroy all opposition, demonstrate His glory throughout all of creation, and ultimately reign as all in all. Far more than repairing the breach in His plan caused by Adam, the plan was formulated to subdue Satan's challenge through the fall and redemption of man. In the process, the church demonstrates God's glory as His vessels of mercy and joint-heirs with Christ.

Knowing the end helps us understand the beginning and the present. In fact the key distinction between the two paradigms is revealed exactly at this point: God's plan for creation was formed with the intention of a final, glorious end rather than a return to the way things began. Like a telescope peering intently across the span of space and time, from eternity past God set His sights on the future "summing up . . . all things in Christ, things in the heavens and things upon the earth." This future summation in Christ is the key to understanding "the anxious longing of the creation" and the object for which it "waits eagerly" (Romans 8:19). The Master's plan is not simply to regain the paradise that was lost at the fall. The "unification of a divided universe"[12] is the ultimate goal of "the mystery of His will."

The drama of creation was completely written before the stage was even set. Before the beginning of creation, God had an end in view. Creation's story will end according to the Master's plan at the final consummation when all enemies will be subjected under the feet of Christ, the kingdom will be handed over to the Father,

[12] Bruce, F.F., *The Epistles to the Colossians, to Philemon, and to the Ephesians (New International Commentary on the New Testament)*, Wm. B. Eerdmans Publishing Company, 1984, p. 261–262.

and God will reign as all in all for eternity. When the drama of all time comes to an end and the closing credits roll, all of creation will see the glory of the Creator.

THE CREATOR'S PURPOSE
IN ACTION

6

A bedrock truth of the Christian faith is that the Creator's ultimate purpose for His creation is to bring Himself glory. God certainly loves His children and has plans for their welfare, but His sovereign plan for history takes precedence. His plan permits evil, suffering, and difficulties to persist for a short time in order to accomplish His eternal purpose. Resting on this truth, the old earth worldview is in conjunction with the eternal scope of God's purpose.

This world was not created as an unblemished paradise, but rather as a stage on which God's perfect plan would play out. The trials and difficulties of this life are not in opposition to His intent, but rather part of a plan set in motion before creation began and Adam sinned. Historical truth revealed in the pages of Scripture testifies to the primacy of God's purpose as His plan unfolds in the lives of His people.

Joseph: God's Plan Unfolding

Joseph provides a clear illustration of the Perfect Purpose Paradigm. Joseph was a righteous man in whom God's plan was unfolding. The lineage of Christ would pass through Joseph, and moreover, God would use Joseph to provide for the preservation of Christ's forebears in Egypt.

Although he was innocent, Joseph experienced considerable suffering and evil in his life. Joseph's brothers were legitimately guilty of a grievous act of injustice against him. Their evil action brought Joseph years of unjust suffering and trials. Through it all, Joseph remained innocent, unjustly suffering at the hands of people who wished him harm. Yet in the end, Joseph understood the bigger picture. What his brothers had intended for evil, God had intended for good (Genesis 50:20). God was working in the circumstances of his life according to His plan to accomplish a greater good.

In the same way, God allows all of His children to endure sufferings for a time in order to bring about a greater good, all according to the Master's plan. This is the biblical answer to the problem of suffering. Our sovereign God is working all things together to accomplish His perfect purpose, one in which He will be glorified through His creation. In the end, He will put away evil for all eternity, and the sufferings of this life will seem incomparable to the glory we will share with Him.

Job: God's Kingdom Vindicated

Typical Sunday school lessons on Job teach that we are tested in order to become more spiritually mature or to learn patience. On occasion the sovereignty of God over the natural world is taught, but there is also a cosmic significance to Job's ordeal. Job's story is a microcosm that illustrates the Creator's larger purpose for the history of humanity. When we peek behind the veil into the spiritual realm, we see how a cosmic battle ensued in the painful experience of Job. The life of Job is a case study that encapsulates the "Drama of Creation."

Job was a thoroughly faithful follower of God. His troubles began when God piqued Satan's interest, "Have you considered my servant Job?" (Job 1:8). Satan responded that Job was only faithful because God was good to him; take away the blessings and Job would reject God. Here we see the mindset of Satan and perhaps the flawed reasoning behind Satan's rebellion. His answer reveals a deep misunderstanding and undervaluing of God's dominion. The accuser claimed that people only follow God because He is good to them. He implied that God must buy favor from His children. So in this field test, God demonstrates to Satan that He is worthy to be followed not just for what He does, but more importantly, because of who He is. Through Job, God demonstrates that His people choose to follow him because of His worth, not because of the blessings it brings. God reigns because His kingdom is worthy of all glory.

Clearly, if God's intent was to minimize or prevent suffering, He could have prevented the suffering Job experienced. Of course God could have simply refused the request of Satan. But that was not His plan. Note that it was God's provocation that initiated Satan's request to afflict Job. Job's suffering was not due to his sin—God started the whole mess by pointing out that "there is no one like him on the earth, a blameless and upright man" (Job 1:8; 2:3). Far from blaming fallen man or even Satan for Job's suffering, the Scripture says that Job suffered from "evil that the LORD had brought on him" (42:11). Satan was allowed to inflict suffering on Job so that God would be glorified and the adversary's accusation falsified.

Seeing Job as a microcosm helps us understand how God created this world as a stage on which the error of Satan's challenge would be demonstrated. Job gives us insight into why Satan was allowed to harass and inflict suffering on God's image-bearers. Job helps us understand why God did not choose to prevent suffering at all costs. Perhaps Job served as a reminder to Satan that his attempt to usurp God's authority and acquire His throne was spurious.

Like Job, the people of God must choose to follow God even when difficulties abound, proving that Satan is wrong and that his kingdom will not prevail. Rather than turning on God in fickle faithfulness, the child of God must continue to run hard after the King.

Pharaoh: God's Power Demonstrated

Israel's bondage in Egypt provides another excellent example of the Perfect Purpose Paradigm in action. The Master's plan is seen in the predestined suffering of His people and the demonstration of His sovereign power in their deliverance. Like Job, this brief period in the history of Israel illustrates what the Perfect Purpose Paradigm posits for all of human history. In this epochal event we see a vivid picture of God's purpose for creation. Each act in the drama of creation is played out in Israel's deliverance.

Unjust Suffering

Before the children of Israel ever existed, they were predestined to innocently suffer. This fact alone dispels the flawed theology of young earth creationism. From the very beginning of God's covenant with Abram, God made the plan for His people clear: "God said to Abram, 'Know for certain that your descendants will be strangers in a land that is not theirs, where they will be enslaved and oppressed four hundred years. But I will also judge the nation whom they will serve, and afterward they will come out with many possessions,'" (Genesis 15:13–14).

From the start, God had a plan for His chosen people. They were destined to endure four centuries of unjust suffering at the hands of the Egyptians, but their suffering would eventually lead to glory. God had provided for the survival of His people by elevating Joseph to the pinnacle of Pharaoh's administration. The children of Israel experienced blessings and favor in the eyes of Pharaoh until he died and "a new king arose over Egypt, who did not know Joseph" (Exodus 1:8). To prevent them from rising up and overpowering the Egyptians, the children of Israel were enslaved.

Many generations of Israelites lived and died knowing only bondage as their way of life. Their only hope was the ancient promise to their forefather that God would bring them out when the time was right. But when the years added up and the trials took their toll, their hope of deliverance faded into despair. This was the condition of God's people when Moses first told them that God had heard their cries for help: "they did not listen to Moses on account of their despondency and cruel bondage" (Exodus 6:9).

God's people were despondent and hopeless because of the cruel bondage of their daily existence. Unjust was their suffering. They had committed no crime in the eyes of man, nor had they done any wrong before God to deserve enslavement to the Egyptians.[1] Rather than their sins, it was God's plan that brought their suffering. "Despondency and cruel bondage" were part of God's plan.

A Perfect Purpose

A striking contrast between the two creation paradigms is revealed in the narrative of Pharaoh and the bondage of Israel. The Perfect Paradise Paradigm reasons that all suffering is either directly or indirectly related to sin. Had Adam not sinned, there would have been no need for a covenant or atonement. On this

---

[1] That is what sets this time apart from the later periods of captivity that Israel would endure. The later times of captivity were always a judgment for their lack of faithfulness. Because the Israelites would later fail to heed God's warning to turn from their evil ways, they would suffer slavery to their enemies. But in this instance, the children of Israel were in Egypt solely because of God's plan. Recall how they had gotten there: it began with a blessing.

point both paradigms agree. However, the paradigms differ on who is ultimately responsible for Israel's captivity. Young earth creationism presumes that Adam is ultimately responsible because his sin brought about all human suffering. God then orchestrated events to recover from the fall of man by establishing His covenant with Abraham and laying the foundation for atonement through Christ. This was done to restore creation to its original intended purpose—fellowship between the Creator and His image-bearers.

As pleasant as this idea is, however, it fails to account for the events recorded in Scripture regarding the Jewish captivity in Egypt. In fact, nowhere is the Perfect Purpose Paradigm more clearly illustrated than in these events. Nowhere in this passage does God shirk away from responsibility for the suffering of His people. He never assigns blame to humanity. It was not the fall of Adam that led to Israel's captivity. It was not the evil intent of Pharaoh that caused them to suffer. It was God who appointed Pharaoh for this specific purpose according to His Master Plan: "For the Scripture says to Pharaoh, 'For this very purpose I raised you up, to demonstrate my power in you, and that my name might be proclaimed throughout the whole earth,'" (Romans 9:17).

The children of Israel were predestined to suffer for one reason: that God could demonstrate His glory to His people and all creation.[2] The Creator's plan for creation included giving Pharaoh authority over God's people for the express purpose of using Pharaoh to demonstrate God's power and nature throughout all of creation. It was neither directly nor indirectly due to the sin of Adam that Pharaoh oppressed God's people. Israel's time of captivity was sovereignly ordained in the eternal plan of God because it was God's ultimate purpose to demonstrate His glory.

---

[2] Note how strikingly similar "this very purpose" is to the administration of Creator's mystery revealed in Ephesians 3:8–11.

That God's concern was revealing His glory is also apparent in His preparatory remarks to Moses. "God spoke further to Moses and said to him, 'I am the LORD; and I appeared to Abraham, Isaac, and Jacob, as God Almighty, but by My name, LORD, I did not make Myself known to them. . . . Then I will take you for My people, and I will be your God; and you shall know that I am the LORD your God, who brought you out from under the burdens of the Egyptians,'" (Exodus 6:2–3, 7).

Through this epochal event of salvation from Egypt, God revealed Himself in a fundamentally new way. While He made His strength and power known to Abraham, Isaac, and Jacob, they did not know Him as Redeemer and Deliverer. Through this historical event in Egypt He demonstrated previously unrevealed aspects of His person, His ways of relating to His people, and the nature of His plan for creation for the first time.

It is important to recognize that neither the magnitude nor number of plagues were due to the evil belligerence of Pharaoh. God made His intended purpose for the plagues and deliverance of Israel emphatic and clear: He was demonstrating His glorious power to the pagan Egyptians as well. "But I will harden Pharaoh's heart that I may multiply My signs and My wonders in the land of Egypt. When Pharaoh does not listen to you, then I will lay My hand on Egypt and bring out My hosts, My people the sons of Israel, from the land of Egypt by great judgments. The Egyptians shall know that I am the LORD, when I stretch out My hand on Egypt and bring out the sons of Israel from their midst" (Exodus 7:3–5).

God had brought His people to this point for a specific purpose: "that I may multiply My signs and My wonders in the land of Egypt." He took direct responsibility for the signs and the wonders in Egypt just as He had predestined the Israelites to bondage. Clearly God was taking responsibility for the difficulty and suffering brought about by His choice in order to demonstrate His glorious power.

Although it is perhaps a subtle distinction, it is vital to recognize that God intentionally raised Pharaoh up and planned the suffering of both the Israelites and Egyptians expressly for the purpose of demonstrating His glory to the whole earth. Pharaoh was certainly guilty before God and justly deserved the punishment God inflicted upon him, but the point here is not the punishment of Pharaoh for his guilt. God does not justify His action by saying Pharaoh or the Egyptian people brought this on themselves—it is expressly for the purpose of making His glory known. God did not merely take advantage of the opportunity provided by the fall to use the suffering for His glory. Pharaoh was purposely elevated to this position and time in history to show God's power. Indeed, Israel was also predestined to suffer affliction because it was the means God chose to accomplish His purpose.

This same truth relates to the plan of atonement. It was not that Christ was sent to rescue His people simply out of compassion for their plight while in bondage to sin. Nor did God formulate the plan of atonement in advance simply because He foresaw the sin of man. Much more, atonement was the original intent of God's plan in order to accomplish His eternal purpose—the demonstration of His glorious name. Pharaoh serves to illustrate how God is at work to reveal His glory through the entire drama of creation.

Judgment on Their Gods

Since the ultimate purpose for creation is to glorify the Creator, one means to that end is the judgment of Satan and his rebellious cohorts. This aspect of God's plan is also evident in the Exodus story, for the final plague had a two-fold purpose. God said that He would kill the first-born of man and beast "and against all the gods of Egypt I will execute judgments—I am the LORD" (Exodus 12:12). This aspect of the plagues was so significant that it is reiterated in recollection in Numbers 33:4. Not only was God delivering his people and showing His power, He was also executing judgment on the spiritual rulers behind this evil, earthly kingdom. In the same way, God is delivering His children from bondage to the ruler of this world while at the same time judging those rulers. Through the drama of creation, the Creator is glorifying Himself and judging those spiritual rulers that have risen up against Him.

Final Consummation

While it is true that God foreordained the suffering of Israel to accomplish His purpose, the story has a happy ending for the Israelites. It was God's predestined purpose to subject the nation of Israel to futility and bondage for a brief time, yet with the hope of deliverance. Before the captivity had begun, God promised Abram that He would judge the captors of Israel and His children would come out of captivity with many possessions (Genesis 15:13–14).

In fulfillment of this promise, judgment on the house of Pharaoh did not end with the plagues. After the children of Israel left Egypt, God sent them on a meandering path to make it look to Pharaoh as if "they [were] wandering aimlessly in the land" (Exodus 14:3). God's purpose for Pharaoh had not quite been completed, for God said "I will harden Pharaoh's heart, and he will chase after them; and I will be honored through Pharaoh and all his army, and the Egyptians will know that I am the LORD," (Exodus 14:4; also 14:17–18). Fulfilling the promise to Abram, God finally judged the captors of Israel, delivered His people with many possessions, and in so doing, brought glory to Himself.

There is a strong parallel between the suffering of Israel while under captivity in Egypt and the suffering of God's children living in a world under the dominion of Satan (Ephesians 2:1–2). Like the children of Israel in Egypt, our momentary afflictions give rise to hope for an eternal glory in the plan of God. Indeed, the ruler of this world has been judged through the atoning death of Christ on the cross, and we are "joint-heirs" with Christ. As Israel's bondage in Egypt demonstrates, God's plan for His people includes suffering for a short time and for a definite purpose, yet with a blessed hope in the consummation.

Cosmic Connection

God's purpose for this event in history is clear in retrospect. He was not solely motivated by a desire to relieve the oppression of His people. That had been accomplished with their deliverance. Indeed it was His plan that brought on the oppression of His people. Much more, God's concern was to demonstrate His glory to all people. For that reason He further hardened Pharaoh's heart and the hearts of the Egyptians even after the deliverance had been accomplished. The Master's plan was to permit His people to suffer for a time in order to accomplish His purpose. Through delivering His people from suffering, He judged the rulers and authorities that opposed His kingdom and demonstrated His glory.

This brief event in the history of Israel encapsulates the purpose of God for all of the history of His creation. In their song of praise to their Deliverer, Moses and the people said,

> Thy right hand, O Lord, is majestic in power, Thy right hand O Lord, shatters the enemy. And in the greatness of Thine excellence Thou dost overthrow those who rise up against Thee. . . . Who is like Thee among the gods, O Lord? . . . In Thy lovingkindness Thou hast led the people whom Thou hast redeemed; In Thy strength Thou hast guided them to Thy holy habitation. . . . Thou wilt bring them and plant them in the mountain of Thine inheritance, the place O Lord, which Thou has made for Thy dwelling, the sanctuary, O Lord, which Thy hands have established. The Lord shall reign forever and ever. (Exodus 15:6–7,11,13,17–18)

God demonstrates His mighty power through His people to all of creation as He overthrows those who rise up against Him. By His strength He guides His people through this life toward a promised, eternal dwelling prepared for them where He shall reign forever. That was the purpose of God for Israel, and it is the purpose of God for the entire drama of creation.

The embodiment of the Perfect Purpose Paradigm is evident in the direct parallel between Pharaoh and the children of Israel to Satan and the people of God. In both cases, God empowered an evil dominion in order to accomplish His purpose. God raised up Pharaoh "for this very purpose . . . to demonstrate My power in You, and that My name might be proclaimed throughout the whole earth" (Romans 9:17). Even though it meant bondage and suffering for His people, God empowered Pharaoh's kingdom for the express purpose of demonstrating His power. God's plan for His people permitted bondage in Egyptian slavery in order to deliver His people and in the process demonstrate His power, judge the gods, and proclaim His name throughout the whole earth. The brief suffering of Israel led to enduring blessings because they came out with many possessions on the way to the Promised Land. In the end, Pharaoh and the gods of Egypt were judged and never again tormented God's people. It was not the sin of the people but the plan of the Creator that brought this about.

Like Pharaoh, Satan was empowered after his rebellion for the very purpose of demonstrating God's glory to all of creation in heaven and on earth. Like Pharaoh, Satan oppresses God's people and keeps them in bondage for a time until God sends His deliverer. God allows His people to suffer in bondage to sin under the authority of Satan in order to redeem His people and demonstrate His glory to the people of the earth and the rulers in the heavenly places. Like Pharaoh, Satan's judgment was deferred, and instead God raised him up for the distinct purpose of demonstrating His power in him, that His name would be proclaimed throughout the heavens and the earth.

Like the Israelites, the sufferings of this present time are not comparable to the glorious inheritance and eternal home that awaits us. In the end, justice will be executed and Satan will never again contend with God's people. This truth lies at the heart of the Perfect Purpose Paradigm.[3]

The Patience of God with Pharaoh

It is interesting to observe that the sin of Pharaoh is like the sin of Satan: he rebelled against the authority of God and considered his throne superior to God's kingdom. Pharaoh even said, "Who is the LORD that I should obey His voice to let Israel go? I do not know the LORD, and besides, I will not let Israel go," (Exodus 5:2). In essence, Pharaoh was exerting his supremacy over all other gods, claiming that no one had authority over him.

One might well ask why Pharaoh was given so many chances. God could have dealt swiftly with Him to deliver His people, but instead Moses was repeatedly sent to appeal for the release of the captives. Why did God allow the persecution of His people to persist while He continued to extend opportunities to Pharaoh, knowing that Pharaoh would still harden his heart? Was it grace or mercy to give Pharaoh plenty of opportunities to come to his senses (or pile up evidence of guilt)? The only answer is that God allowed Pharaoh to remain in power in order to more distinctly and overwhelmingly show His power and proclaim His name throughout the earth (Exodus 7:14–16).

The same question can be asked regarding God's dealing with Satan after his fall: why does God continue to give Satan opportunities to wreak havoc throughout human history? Why does God prolong His execution of justice against Satan when

---

[3] In addition, Moses was a type of Christ. Moses was "as God" before His people (Exodus 4:16). God delivered His people from suffering and bondage into the land of rest and promise. Just as God instructed Pharaoh through Moses, God is telling Satan through Christ, "Let My people go!"

doing so brings added misery to humanity? Perhaps God is allowing evidence to accumulate to clearly establish for all eternity the superiority of His ways in contrast to His challenger. One fact remains certain: Satan is allowed to persist for a time in order to more distinctly and overwhelmingly show the power and glory of the Creator. Just as He did with Pharaoh, God has allowed Satan "to remain in order to show you [His] power, and in order to proclaim [His] name through all the earth."

Legion: God's Judgment Deferred

The problem of suffering begs the question as to why Satan was allowed to exercise authority on earth and bring travail to humanity. Although Satan and the fallen angels rebelled against God, the Creator chose to delay the execution of justice against them. Indeed, they have been granted some measure of influence over this fallen world, even though it brings peril to God's people. Yet we can be confident that God's plan ensures that in the end, justice will be executed upon Satan and the fallen angels. The fallen angels know the day is coming and they know what the day will hold. This fact is made evident by the encounter between Jesus and Legion.

The story of Jesus and the man possessed by the group of demons named "Legion" is a well-known Sunday school lesson. Pigs running off a cliff into the sea make for a vivid mental picture and an entertaining object lesson about the person and power of Jesus. Not as well known, however, is the subtle implication of this event that relates to the final judgment of fallen angels.

When Jesus entered the country of the Gerasenes, He came upon the man possessed by Legion. Legion knew that their days were numbered and their judgment was coming; but they also knew that the execution of that judgment had been deferred. Knowing the time had not yet come, they asked Jesus, "Have you come here to torment us before the time?" (Matthew 8:29). They did not ask *if* they were going to be judged. Even though they knew it had not yet come, they knew the judgment would come. In no way did they challenge the authority of Jesus to execute judgment. Nor did they question the justice of doing it immediately. Their dialogue with Jesus indicates they knew Jesus was the Son of God; that He had authority to immediately execute judgment on them, and that such judgment would have been just.

Recognizing Jesus as the "Son of the Most High God," Legion said, "I implore You by God, do not torment me!" (Mark 5:7). Luke records that "They were imploring Him not to command them to go away into the abyss" (Luke 8:31). Instead of tormenting them and sending them into the abyss, which was clearly within the authority of the Son of God to do, He honored their request and sent them into a herd of swine. A subtle truth in this story is that Jesus acted consistently with the Father when He deferred their judgment. What is evident from this encounter between Jesus and Legion is that they knew their day of judgment was coming, and although it had not yet arrived, they knew what the outcome would be.

Jesus' response to Legion has important implications on the problem of suffering and evil. Jesus did not immediately banish them, but instead let them continue on. These demons would not have been able to inflict any further suffering if Jesus had sent them to the abyss rather than granting their request. While we can only speculate about the activities of Legion after parting company with Jesus, we can assume that when Jesus granted the stay of execution to Legion, He allowed the possibility that they could once again cause suffering as they had already done. Christ chose not to prevent evil and suffering in this case when He granted the request of Legion. Legion illustrates the biblical perspective on God's purpose for creation: He permits evil to persist for a time in order to accomplish His eternal purpose.

Legion's deferred judgment illustrates the Creator's wider response to the rebellion of Satan. The Creator would have been fully within the bounds of righteousness and justice to immediately destroy Satan and the rebellious angels before he ever created the earth. Yet He didn't. Perhaps the Creator gave Satan a fair shot to prove his claim to the throne. The Serpent was indeed given permission to enter the garden of Eden and tempt the Creator's image-bearers. Having won the battle in the Garden, the adversary was given dominion over the whole earth. In fact, only God incarnate conquered the power of Satan and his kingdom that was established on earth. Perhaps that is the point the Master was making in the manifold wisdom of His plan. Both the error of their ways and the glory of God's kingdom became apparent to the rebels in the heavenly realms through the Master's plan.

Focal Points

The eternal plan of God has always and unchangingly been to permit and use suffering for a time to accomplish His eternal goals. Suffering is an undeniable, though temporary, part of His "very good" creation through which He is bringing His plan to fruition.

Joseph understood that what people intended for evil in his life, his sovereign God intended for a greater good. Job was subjected to great suffering for the express purpose of demonstrating the glory of God and the superiority of His kingdom. Likewise, Pharaoh was raised up for the express purpose of demonstrating God's glory through subjecting God's people to centuries of despair and bondage. Legion also shows us that God defers the execution of judgment on evil spiritual forces until His chosen time, even if it may entail a time of suffering for His people. In each case, we see God's plan unfolding through the events of history for the purpose of demonstrating His glory. This creation suffers for a time, not because of the will of the creature but by the will of the Creator. The blessed hope is that our brief sufferings in this life are not comparable to the eternal glory that we will share with the Creator (Romans 8:18–23).

Admittedly, the notion that suffering is part of God's plan is uncomfortable if we are accustomed to blaming Adam for all suffering. But the Bible clearly testifies that from the beginning, His plan has been for humanity to suffer for a time in order to demonstrate His glory through our liberation for all eternity.

So what does theology have to do with the age of the earth? According to the Perfect Purpose Paradigm, the finished creation was "very good" because it set the stage for God's unfolding plan. Yes, there had been generations of animals pass from the stage before man arrived on the scene. Yes, the struggle for survival in nature may be unseemly from our perspective. But the Father's perspective is larger. It may be an uncomfortable notion that God's perfect plan allowed suffering in His "very good" creation, but the Father has a higher purpose than ensuring creature comforts.

This world is perfectly suited for the Master's perfect purpose. God is working out His plan to address rebellion in the heavens, do away with evil for eternity, demonstrate His glory for all eternity to all of creation, and reign forever as all in all. In light of that end rather than an idyllic beginning, the world was indeed "very good." With this understanding we must now turn to an analysis of the natural world to compare the veracity of our two paradigms.

PART 3

THE WORLD BEFORE THE FALL

A DAY IN THE LIFE OF ADAM

Having discussed the purpose of God for which He created the world, our attention now turns to understanding what the world was like before the fall. The material world was indeed created "very good," perfectly fit for the perfect purpose of the Creator. This chapter will consider what the "very good" world must have been like from the perspective of God's purpose for an ancient creation.

Prime Real Estate

Following the orderly description of the creation week in Genesis 1:1–2:4, the creation narrative is revisited with the focus turning to man's relation to the Creator and the created world. The Creator had prepared a special place for Adam and Eve: "The Lord God planted a garden toward the east, in Eden; and there He placed the man whom He had formed" (Genesis 2:8).

Genesis 2:8–17 goes on to describe a how God graciously provided for his image-bearers in a bountiful and beautiful garden paradise. It was a lush home abundantly supplied with water and adorned with precious stones. If ever there was a prime piece of real estate, it was the garden of Eden.

Having finished the preparations, God gave dominion over the garden to man that he might rule as an obedient, joyous act of worship. There were discoveries and interactions of many sorts awaiting Adam in the garden. The garden was full of beautiful sights and stimulation for his appetites. Apart from the beauty and bounty, there was work to engage his mind and body. For his spiritual development, there was a wide range of latitude for freedom, but there was one solitary restriction.

The preparation of the garden was distinct from the creation of vegetation throughout the earth which God created on the third day. According to Genesis 2:8–9, the garden was not "created," but was instead "planted." God did not create mature trees in the garden but rather "out of the ground the LORD God caused to grow every tree . . ." God certainly could have created mature trees or miraculously accelerated the growth of the garden, but the Bible does not say He did that. Proper exegesis and a plain reading of the passage suggest that God planted a garden using normal providence.[1] Interestingly, the Hebrew terminology and grammar also indicate that the garden was planted after the creation of Adam.[2] Taken together, this indicates that a significant amount of time may have passed between the creation of Adam and his taking up residence in the garden. The fact that Eve was created after "God took the man and put him into the garden" helps us understand Adam's response when he first awoke to meet Eve and exclaimed: "At long last!"[3]

---

[1] Normal providence indicates that God caused it to grow through the provision of His sunshine and His rain using His normal means which He created. The use of normal means in no way minimizes the dependence of the process on God's providence.

[2] The pluperfect tense of the clause "whom He had formed" concluding verse eight indicates that the planting of the garden occurred after the creation of Adam. See Mathews, Kenneth A., *The New American Commentary, Genesis 1–11:26*, Broadman & Holman Publishers, 1996, p. 200.

[3] Hugh Ross points out in *Creation and Time* that the Hebrew phrase "This is now" in 2:23 can be rendered "at long last."

Many of misperceptions about life before the fall can be traced to the common notion that the entire earth was like the garden of Eden. Yet the Scriptures indicate that the garden was a unique location not necessarily like the rest of the earth. The phrase "a garden toward the east, in Eden" indicates that the garden was located within a larger surrounding geographic region known as "Eden." A divinely prepared habitat for Adam and Eve, the garden was amply supplied with "every tree that [was] pleasing to sight and good for food." (Genesis 2:9). Water was abundantly supplied to the garden by a river flowing out of Eden and forming four tributaries.[4] It was adorned with lush beauty, precious metals, and jewels. Imagine how spectacular the garden must have been! The garden of Eden had all Adam could want or need.

God prepared a special place for Adam that was distinct from the rest of the earth. Much like a nature preserve or zoological park, Eden was an ideal habitat that was set apart as the abode for God's image-bearers. A common presumption is that all animal species were present with Adam in the garden, but the Bible simply does not state or imply that polar bears, kangaroos, or "herbivorous lions" were in the garden with Adam. Perhaps while preparing the garden for His image-bearers, the Creator populated the garden with animals specifically chosen to interact with Adam within the confines of the garden preserve.[5]

Eden was much different from the world around it. The garden was specially prepared for its new occupants with no weeds, thorns, or harmful animals.[6] The tranquil nature of the garden

---

[4] Two of the named rivers, the Tigris and Euphrates Rivers, are identifiable today but the identity of the others is not known.

[5] Dawson, J. W., *The Origin of the World According to Revelation and Science*, Harper & Brothers, Publishers, New York, 1877, p. 237–238.

[6] Ramm, Bernard, *Christian View of Science and Scripture*, Wm. B. Eerdmans Publishing Co., 1954, p. 233. Just as the angel barred the couple's entrance to the garden after the fall, God could have enforced a perimeter around the garden to prevent harmful animals from entering the sanctuary of Eden.

does not imply that every animal on the planet was an herbivore. Humans could have peacefully coexisted with certain animals in the garden while harmful beasts freely roamed elsewhere. Likewise, the absence of thorns and weeds in the specially prepared garden does not mean there were no thorns or weeds anywhere on the planet—they simply were not present in the confines of the garden paradise.

Biblical prophecy speaks of a future time when there will be no harmful animals on God's holy mountain (Isaiah 11:9; 65:25). Israel is also promised that harmful beasts will be eliminated from their land if they are faithful (Leviticus 26:6).[7] Interestingly, these statements speak of a limited location. A similar situation characterizes the garden of Eden. Eden was prepared as a unique and ideal habitat for man according to the Creator's purposes.

The Two Trees

Two unique trees are distinguished from among all the plants in the garden. Symbolically representing the prominent role it played, the Tree of Life was located "in the midst of the garden." Close by was the Tree of the Knowledge of Good and Evil. God prominently displayed these two trees in the center of the garden as a clear statement of the choice set before man.

Adam was instructed in no uncertain terms regarding the Tree of Knowledge: "in the day that you eat from it you shall surely die" (verse 17).[8] God set a choice before Adam in the center of

---

[7] This point is reinforced in Leviticus 26:7 where God also promises to Israel that "you will chase your enemies and they will fall before you by the sword." Clearly although there are no harmful animals or death in their land, there is death by the sword to Israel's enemies.

[8] One may argue that Adam must have witnessed the physical death of animals prior to the fall. Although Adam and Eve could have conceivably understood spiritual death as separation from God's fellowship, they would have had to witness physical death for the commandment to have meaning.

his world: he could choose to obey and eat the fruits of life or he could disobey God and be consumed by the curse of death. The same message was spoken through Moses when God said, "See, I am setting before you today a blessing and a curse: the blessing, if you will listen to the commandments of the Lord your God, which I am commanding you today; and the curse, if you do not listen to the commandments of the Lord your God, but turn aside from the way which I am commanding you today" (Deut. 11: 26–28). Adam chose the latter and as God promised, he died that very day.

Although both spiritual and physical death came to Adam as a result of sin, the immediate consequence of sin was spiritual death. In New Testament terminology, the very instant that Adam ate from the tree, "sin effected [his] death" and he died spiritually (Romans 7:13). His spiritual death was manifested in the recognition of his nakedness and the immediate broken fellowship with God. Sin also produced physical death when God banished Adam and Eve from the garden to prevent their access to the Tree of Life. In doing so, God withdrew His provision for sustaining Adam's life and sin led to his physical death over nine hundred years later.

Standing in stark contrast to the Tree of Life was the Tree of the Knowledge of Good and Evil. This tree's presence in the garden is significant to the problem of suffering and evil. With all the liberty that God had granted to Adam—giving him dominion over all creation and allowing him to eat of any green plants he saw—there was only one exception: he could not eat from the Tree of the Knowledge. God didn't burden Adam with a book of laws. The Tree of Knowledge was the single prohibition set in the midst of God's bountiful provision. Adam had boundless liberty with the exception of this one choice set before him—life or death. The potential for Adam to choose disobedience indicates that the created world was fashioned to allow free will and temptation. Evil was real, and evil was a choice. God had chosen to allow evil in the material world because it already existed in the heavenly realm. God could have chosen to prevent evil in the creation, but that was not His plan.

Mortality of Man

Adam was not explicitly told that he had to eat from the Tree of Life to live, so evidently it wasn't necessary for survival. The presence of the Tree of Life in the midst of the garden symbolized constant access to God's provision for eternal life. Adam had a tangible demonstration that life comes only from the Creator and through the Creator. Absent the provision of God, man has no eternal life. This principle is taught throughout the Scriptures: eternal life is only made available from and through God, who alone possesses immortality (1 Timothy 6:16). Immortality was not innate with Adam, but was a gift imparted to him from God.[9] Eternal life for Adam was contingent upon God's sustenance.[10]

The Tree of Life was given to the first couple to symbolize God's provision for the sustenance of their lives. After the fall, the couple was banished from the Garden and an angel barred their access to the Tree of Life. The angel was a tangible reminder that they now needed a new means of access to the source of eternal life. This also indicates the symbolic nature of the tree, for access to the tree would not have been possible for the dispersed descen-

---

[9] It is reasonable to assume that if man were created immortal, there would be no need for the tree to have been in the garden.

[10] God told Adam, "From any tree of the garden you may eat freely; but from the tree of the knowledge of good and evil you shall not eat, for in the day that you eat from it you will surely die" (Genesis 2:16–17). This command only states what would happen if Adam disobeyed—it does not necessarily imply that He would live forever by not eating that fruit. Glenn Morton illustrates this distinction well in his essay "Death Before the Fall," (http://home.entouch.net/dmd/death.htm, accessed April 11, 2005). As he explains, if someone eats a toadstool, they will die from liver failure within 24 hours. But for someone to state that if you eat a toadstool, in that day you will die, that doesn't mean you will live forever if you don't eat a toadstool.

dents of Adam had they not fallen. If there was only one Tree of Life and it granted immortality, then the subsequent generations who obediently filled the earth would not have had access to the tree.[11]

The Tree of Life symbolically represents the provision of life given by God to those who appropriate it according to His requirements. In exactly the same way, we appropriate God's gift of eternal life by receiving the life given through Christ, "for in him we live, and move, and have our being" (Acts 17:28 KJV). Calvin taught that Adam was not immortal; stating that Adam's "earthly life truly would have been temporal; yet he would have passed into heaven without death, and without injury" had he not sinned. Prior to the fall of Adam, death was possible, but not inevitable.[12] Enoch and Elijah are two examples of men who did not die yet were not innately immortal. Perhaps that is the pattern that Adam, Eve, and all their descendents would have followed if the fall had not occurred.

One might suggest that the Tree of Life foreshadows another tree in the Scriptures, the tree upon which Christ died to give us life. When Adam and Eve's access to the tree was prevented after the fall, another provision was needed whereby man could obtain eternal life, which was made available through the death of Christ on the cross. The first picture of the vicarious death of Christ is given when God slays an innocent animal to provide a covering for the nakedness of Adam and Eve, nakedness that represented the sin that separated them from God.

Although the immortality of Adam is an open theological question, it is not a significant doctrinal issue. However, it is a necessary condition for the Perfect Paradise Paradigm. For if

---

[11] Munday, John C., "Creature Mortality: From Creation or the Fall?" *Journal of the Evangelical Theological Society*, Volume 35, No. 1, March 1992, p. 51–68.

[12] Chafer, L. S., *Systematic Theology*, Dallas Seminary Press, 1975.

Adam was not immortal before the fall, then neither were animals immortal before the fall. It still remains that even if Adam were indeed immortal before the fall, that fact in no way implies original animal immortality.[13]

The Dominion Mandate

Adam was placed in the garden to work, grow, learn, and experience intimate fellowship with God. As Adam interacted with the Creator and the creation, God was revealing His glory to Adam and teaching Adam his place in the creation. God demonstrated that He was the source of life and all good things through the bountiful sustenance of the garden and the Tree of Life. Adam experienced spiritual fulfillment like no one other than Christ as he walked and talked with God. God also gave significant responsibilities to Adam that he might serve God and experience firsthand the beauty and majesty of God's creation. He was entrusted with stewardship over all of creation—dominion over the earth and the animal kingdom.

Adam and Eve were charged by their Creator to be fruitful and multiply, fill the earth and subdue it, and rule over the fish of the sea, the birds of the air, and every living thing that moves on the earth (Genesis 1:28). This instruction is typically called the "dominion mandate." Proponents of young earth creationism assume the somewhat ironic position that this mandate required Adam to exercise authority through benign interaction with every

---

[13] This point was made in the 19th century by T. S. Ackland who wrote, "Though, then, it seems by no means improbable that Adam, if he had not fallen, would have been exempt from the dissolution of the body, yet this is not absolutely certain, and even if it were certain, his case would be an exceptional one: no inference as to the immortality of the animal creation could have been drawn from it." Taken from "The Story of Creation as told by Theology and by Science," London, Society for Promoting Christian Knowledge, 1890.

animal species on the planet. The interaction had to be benign because there was no potential danger from the exercise of this mandate with harmful animals. Adam was supposedly not like a lion tamer at the circus—no force or exertion was needed to carry out this mandate because there was no potential for harm, suffering, or danger.

Like the assumption that there were exactly three wise men at Christ's birth, this idyllic vision is read into the silence of Scripture. It is likely that the garden was populated with specially chosen animals, not necessarily every species. Some scholars have noted that not all animals were included in the dominion mandate. If the *bhemah* created on the fifth day and explicitly called out in the dominion mandate were herbivorous animals, then "the carnivorous creatures are not mentioned, and possibly were not included in man's dominion."[14] Even if this distinction does not hold, Adam did not necessarily interact directly with every created animal while he was in the garden of Eden. What Adam learned in the confines of the garden prepared him for his work to come.

Subdue the Earth

Adam's first specific instructions were given in a context of blessing: "God blessed them; and God said to them, 'Be fruitful and multiply, and fill the earth, and subdue it; and rule over the fish of the sea and over the birds of the sky and over every living thing that moves on the earth'" (Genesis 1:28).

---

[14] Dawson, J. W., p. 231–232. Dawson points out that *bhemah* is typically associated with cattle or domesticated animals and is used when it is necessary to make a distinction with predacious or carnivorous animals. Dawson renders the Hebrew compound term *hay'th-eretz* which literally is "animal of the land" as *carnivora*, or carnivorous mammals, p. 232.

Before the fall, Adam was instructed to subdue the earth. Adam was given stewardship over the animal kingdom.[15] The work of subduing is very insightful for establishing a proper paradigm about life before the fall. The word "subdue" found in Genesis 1:28 is the Hebrew word *kābash*, which means to "bring into bondage, keep under, or force."[16] It can also be translated as "to tread down . . . to conquer, subjugate . . . bring into subjection." More force is given by the Hebrew word than the modern reader has come to understand.

Subdue cannot have a benign meaning in that there was an implied opposition from the creation to Adam's efforts to subdue it. Completely apart from the sin of man, "there was a state of travail in nature from the first, which man was empowered to 'subdue' (1:28)."[17]

Here is a point of significant distinction between the two creation paradigms. Essentially, God commanded Adam to overcome or enslave the earth. Far from a harmonious relationship with a benign creation as imagined by the Perfect Paradise Paradigm, the Scripture indicates that there was a need to subdue and rule. Commenting on the Hebrew word for "subdue," the *Theological Wordbook of the Old Testament* says,

---

[15] Even though this labor brought great pleasure to Adam, it reinforced the notion that he was unique. And Adam was alone. God used these tasks as an object lesson to show Adam that there was a greater relationship prepared for him, a unique love found through one uniquely suitable for him. After faithfully exercising his responsibility in the garden and naming all the animals, God put him to sleep and from his rib created Eve. Upon waking, Adam said, "this is now bone of my bone, and flesh of my flesh" (verse 23). Translated literally, he said, "finally, at long last, here is the one for me!" What a beautiful picture Genesis 2 provides for the ideal love relationship God has given His people, an apt metaphor for the relationship between Christ and His church.

[16] R. L. Harris, G. L. Archer, Jr., B. K. Waltke, *Theological Wordbook of the Old Testament*, Moody Press, 1980, p. 430.

[17] Kidner, Derek, *Genesis: An Introduction and Commentary*, Intervarsity Press, 1967, p. 73.

In the OT it means "to make to serve, by force if necessary." Despite recent interpretations of Genesis 1:28 which have tried to make "subdue" mean a responsibility for building up, it is obvious from an overall study of the word's usage that this is not so. *Kābash* assumes that the party being subdued is hostile to the subduer, necessitating some sort of coercion if the subduing is to take place. . . . Therefore "subdue" in Genesis 1:28 implies that creation will not do man's bidding gladly or easily and that man must now bring creation into submission by main strength. It is not to rule man.[18]

Adam was commanded to subdue the earth, and the earth was going to resist and fight back. In order to execute his task, Adam had to work to overcome the resistance of the plant and animal kingdom. There cannot be a benign meaning to this command. Some coercion was needed to overcome the hostile resistance of the plant and animal kingdoms.

Cultivate and Keep

God placed man in the garden with a job to do. While some may think that toil and labor was a consequence of the fall, work was part of Adam's life before the fall. Work did not come about as part of the curse. "Then the LORD God took the man and put him into the garden of Eden to cultivate it and keep it" (Genesis 2:15).

Work was not a command—it was a divine compulsion. The process of work was intended by God to be fulfilling and rewarding. In the original created order this stewardship over creation was a joyful opportunity for man to express gratitude to God and exercise stewardship over the garden. The Hebrew word translated "cultivate" is the same word translated as "worship" in Exodus

---

[18] R. L. Harris, G. L. Archer, Jr., B. K. Waltke, *Theological Wordbook of the Old Testament*, Moody Press, 1980, p. 951.

3:12. Through faithfully toiling in the garden, Adam was express-
ing his submission to the rightful authority of God as Lord over all
creation. Far from frustration, this brought Adam joy.

The necessity of cultivating the garden implies that the garden
was in need of maintenance. God had specially prepared it for its
new inhabitant, but for it to remain in that state would require
faithful tending. The need to cultivate the garden clearly implies
that the garden was not self-sustaining. Some measure of decay or
degeneration before the fall must be implied here. Perhaps while
living outside the garden, Adam had observed what the un-culti-
vated world was like. He appreciated the gift he had been given,
and he understood the need to maintain it.

Adam was also instructed to "keep" the garden. More than
merely maintaining possession, this verb means "to watch or keep
guard from any hostile attack."[19] Much like the need to "subdue
the earth," the instruction to "keep" implies a hostile resistance
to Adam's charge. If there were no tendency for the garden to
become "un-kept," there would have been no reason for Adam
to "keep" it.

Adam took over the responsibility of tending the pristine garden, originally planted by God, but he had to work to maintain it.
Although unparalleled in beauty, the garden of Eden was not self-
sustaining nor was it self-perpetuating. Prior to the fall, Adam
faithfully maintained the garden in its pristine state. But after the
fall, Adam was exiled out of the pristinely landscaped garden into
the untamed world where he would have to contend with thorns
and thistles.

This is an easily understood perspective to those familiar with
farming. Farmers who break new ground know that the work is

---

[19] McDonald, Donald, *Biblical Doctrine of Creation and the Fall*, Thomas
Constable and Co., Edinburgh, 1856, Reprinted by Klock & Klock Christian
Publishers, 1984, p. 335.

grueling. They can certainly appreciate the weight of Adam's penalty when he was kicked out of the garden and had to start from scratch. Anyone who has purchased undeveloped land to build a house understands the difficulty of bringing the native weeds under control in the process of establishing a beautiful lawn. It takes work to cultivate and keep. A systemic change in the laws of physics is not necessary to understand the significance of the thorns in the curse (Genesis 3:18). In his fallen state, Adam's behavior would change, his work ethic would deteriorate, and he would have great difficulty "cultivating" and "keeping" the untamed world outside the bounds of the garden.

Adam was intended to enjoy, appreciate, and find great fulfillment in his labor—the curse made the work become a painful chore. In this manner, the fall of man had a devastating impact on the world. Work did not begin after the fall; it became grievous and difficult. Fallen and depraved men became unable to complete the mandate given by God and the entire world suffered.

Focal Points

God set aside a portion of the created world and filled it with bounty and beauty as a residence for His image-bearer. The garden was a place of luscious vegetation, flowing waters, and precious stones. If ever there was a perfectly landscaped location, it was the garden of Eden.

Eden, with all of its unparalleled excellence, stood in sharp contrast to the untamed world around it. Much like the contrast of the two trees set in the center of Adam's world, the garden tangibly demonstrated the delights of God's provision and the blessings that come with obedience. Another sharp contrast existed between Adam and the animals. Adam alone had a moral capacity and the freedom to resist urges both external and internal. He alone was subject to moral considerations with the capacity for intimacy with his Creator. It is a fully unwarranted leap to extend his dual promise of immortality and moral accountability to the animal inhabitants of the garden paradise.

The situation was quite different for "the animals, with no such capacity and no such charge." Kidner notes that the animals were "in contented bondage to their surroundings, their behavior a product of inborn and incoming urges."[20] The animals were not subject to moral considerations nor were they capable of intimacy with their Creator. There is nothing in the creation narrative to indicate that animals were not subject to injury or death.

Adam walked with God, had a job, and had a perfect wife; life in the garden was "very good." That is, until sin changed everything. Just how extensive the change was after the sin of Adam is a matter of considerable study and debate. Two common misconceptions, however, lead to difficulty. First, it is often assumed that the characteristics of Eden were true of the entire earth. Second, many understand all types of animals were in the garden with Adam and Eve. Recognizing that neither of these assumptions were the case for Eden helps dispel the incorrect presumptions of the Perfect Paradise Paradigm.

---

[20] Kidner, p. 61

TROUBLE IN PARADISE

The movie *Ghostbusters* tells the story of a quartet of renegade scientists who take a stand against an invasion of aliens from another dimension. Armed with their nuclear powered stun guns, they relentlessly pursue the enemy wherever it appears. Just before collectively unleashing their new prototype weapon against a vaporous apparition, Dr. Egon Spenglar (played by Harold Ramis) and Dr. Peter Venkman (played by Bill Murray) are overheard saying:

Spenglar: "There's something very important I forgot to tell you."

Venkman: "What?"

Spenglar: "Don't cross the streams."

Venkman: "Why?"

Spenglar: "That would be bad."

Venkman: "I'm fuzzy on the whole 'good/bad' thing. What do you mean 'bad?'"

Spenglar: "Try to imagine all life as you know it stopping instantaneously and every molecule in your body exploding at the speed of light."

Venkman: "Alright, that's bad. Okay. Alright. Important safety tip."

Being fuzzy about the whole good/bad thing can lead to all sorts of trouble. It is important for us to have a clear understanding about what the Creator meant by "very good." When the implications of the Perfect Paradise Paradigm are closely investigated, several problems with the paradigm arise. It envisions a radically different world that fails the tests of consistency and credibility on both theological and practical grounds. Because neither the revelation found in Scripture nor the revelation found in nature is consistent with the implications of the paradigm, presuming "very good" to mean perfection is perilous.

Cosmic Conflict

It seems like the church has always struggled with the notion of perfection in the heavens. At the turn of the seventeenth century, the church thought that if the heavens had been created "very good," they would be perfect and unchanging. When the eminent mathematician Johannes Kepler set out to make sense of Tycho Brahe's voluminous data on the positions of planets, he assumed that because the heavens were perfect, the planets must move in circular orbits. When he determined—much to his surprise—that the planets moved in elliptical orbits instead of perfect circles, Kepler is said to have asked, "Oh Lord, how could you do anything so imperfect?" Fortunately, Kepler soon realized that his paradigm was in error rather than the natural motion of the planets.

Just three years after Kepler's discovery, Galileo found himself in the hot seat. When he pointed his new telescope at the sun, Galileo saw strange, irregular-shaped smudges on its surface. Because the spots he saw meant the sun was imperfect, Galileo was considered a heretic by the Church. Four hundred years later, many in the church still think it is heresy to believe that the original creation could have been imperfect in any way.

Evidence continues to pile up against the idyllic notion of unchanging perfection in the heavens.[1] Astronomers readily observe that the universe has been undergoing tumult and change since the beginning of creation. For example, colliding galaxies are grand demonstrations of the large scale motion and turbulence of heavenly bodies traveling through space. A fascinating example of this cosmic carnage is "the antennae galaxies," located 63 million light years away. An image from the Hubble Space Telescope shows two long tails that resemble an insect's antenna streaming away from the colliding galactic cores. The close-up image of the colliding cores reveals stellar nurseries birthing new stars in the dense gaseous regions where the galaxies merge (the bright blue knots). Ribbons of matter can also be seen flowing between galaxies locked in a destructive dance orchestrated by the tug of gravity.[2]

In addition to the cosmic carnage of colliding galaxies, nebulae are beautiful reminders of the violent death of individual stars. One particularly beautiful nebula is the Eskimo Nebula—named for its likeness to a face within a furry parka—which was first observed by William Herschel in 1787. Nebulae are the remains of sun-like stars that shed their outer shell of gas as they near the end of their lives. The expanding shell is then illuminated by the intense radiation from the remnant core which creates a wispy apparition of the former star.

Another spectacular celestial event that testifies to the changing nature of the cosmos is a supernova. These occur when giant stars burn out in a true blaze of glory. As a massive star exhausts its fuel, gravity begins to win the tug of war against the outward

---

[1] Young earth creationist leaders extend the notion of perfection beyond the earth to include the heavens since God declared the entire creation "very good."

[2] An image of the Antennae Galaxies can be seen on http://hubblesite.org/newcenter/newsdesk/archive/releases/1997/34/image/a.

push of nuclear fusion and the star collapses under its own weight. When the core collapses into a super-dense mass (e.g. a neutron star or black hole), the outer gas shell explodes so energetically that the supernova might briefly outshine an entire galaxy of stars. Sometimes distant supernovae can be seen even when they are so far away that their entire home galaxy is too dim to be seen.

When we see a star, we do not see it as it is today. The light striking the earth from a star is a recorded message sent from the star long ago. Although light moves so fast that it could orbit the earth seven times in a second, it takes considerable time to traverse the great distances of space. In fact, light from the sun travels for eight minutes before it reaches the earth. This means that we do not see what the sun looks like right now; we see what it looked like eight minutes ago. Furthermore, we are much closer to the sun than we are to the other stars. For instance, it takes over four years for light to reach us from our sun's closest neighboring star. So when a distant supernova is observed, we are seeing the recorded history of a long-ago and far-away display of celestial fireworks.

In 1987 we observed a particularly interesting example of a star that exploded in a neighboring galaxy. Of course the star did not explode in 1987—that was when the light finally reached us after traveling over 100,000,000,000,000,000 miles over 169,000 years! This raises an important question: if the entire universe was created within the last ten thousand years, how does young earth creationism account for an explosion that happened over 169,000 years ago? There would not have been enough time for the light to reach us so the star never could have existed. In other words, what we actually saw was only a stellar mirage implanted in a beam of light in transit to the earth.

When scientists observe a supernova, they observe a physical process undergoing change in a type of celestial laboratory. The history of Supernova 1987A recorded in starlight has helped refine some astrophysical theories while showing others to be in error. Interestingly, the stellar image of the supernova played out exactly as predicted by leading theories of astrophysics. For the Creator to have recorded a false testimony in the starlight, a recording that played out precisely as predicted by the theories of modern physics, simply seems to be a patently deceptive act by God. It would be nothing less than a lie. As if it were a Hollywood movie, Supernova 1987A would be a fictional account of an historical event that never actually happened. And all of this fiction was supposedly written by the Author who commanded us to study His creation to learn about Him.

Because the heavens demonstrate the character of God, starlight with a false history (the appearance of age) indicates that God is deceptive which is contrary to His nature as it is revealed in Scripture. Moreover, like colliding galaxies and nebulae, supernovae provide stunning examples of change and destruction in the cosmos long before Adam corrupted a supposedly perfect and unchanging paradise.

So what is the alternative? The heavens were never perfect and unchanging. Star birth and death have been taking place since the beginning of creation long ago. The faithful "witness in the sky" (Psalm 89:37) tells the story of an ancient creation by an awesome Creator.

Laws of Nature

Nature is sometimes thought of as evil when someone is adversely affected by an "act of God." But the potential for harm does not mean that the laws themselves are innately evil. Natural disasters result from the same laws that the Creator fashioned to provide for His creation. While we may think that nature is evil when it brings devastation, we generally do not consider nature to be evil when our lives are blessed (or at least not harmfully affected) by its operation. This is one reason why so-called "natural evil" is so difficult to address. While the Perfect Paradise Paradigm resolves the difficulty by presuming that the laws of nature were either always beneficial or benign before the fall, the Scriptures offer a different response. Rather than imagining a world radically different from the one in which we live, the Bible presents a Creator who takes credit for creating the same laws of nature that continue to operate according to His purpose as a demonstration of His glory.

Tornadoes

On average, forty-two people are killed each year by tornadoes in the United States. The worst tornado outbreak in United States history occurred in April 1974. When 148 twisters touched down in thirteen states overnight, 330 people were tragically killed and more than 5,000 were injured. Death and destruction on this scale certainly does not seem "very good."

Especially prone are the Midwest and southeastern states that make up "Tornado Alley." During spring, the mountains of the west channel a cool, dry jet stream to the southeast while low atmospheric pressure draws warm, moist air in from the Gulf of Mexico. Massive thunderstorms are spawned where these two air masses collide. Of the roughly 100,000 thunderstorms each year in the United States, about 1,000 tornadoes are typically formed.

Thunderstorms begin with a layer of warm, moist air trapped beneath a layer of cool, dry air. When the stable layer of cool air is disturbed, the warm moist air rises upward, expanding and cooling. As the rising air cools, the moisture condenses, releasing latent heat that warms the surrounding air.[3] The same thermodynamic process that cools a perspiring runner works in reverse when water vapor condenses from the air. This is also what happens when a cold beverage "sweats" on a hot, humid day. Latent heat from the

---

[3] The amount of water vapor that air can contain is a function of temperature: warmer usually contains more water than cooler air.

warm air is transferred to the cool liquid when moisture condenses on the glass. This type of heat transfer in the atmosphere produces a thunderstorm. As heated air accelerates upward at higher and higher speeds, the potential energy of latent heat is converted to kinetic energy and produces wind. When conditions at different altitudes are favorable, humidity and temperature work together to intensify the winds, forming a vertical column of rotating air that becomes a tornado.

Simply put, tornadoes are the natural result of the laws of thermodynamics combined with geography and the atmosphere. When the potential energy of heat becomes kinetic energy in the moving air masses, thunderstorms, tornadoes, and hurricanes may result. So what would a world be like without these storms? For there to be no stormy winds there would have to be no heat transfer between the oceans and the atmosphere and no variation in atmospheric temperature or humidity across the entire earth. But if storms were not possible, then neither would it be possible to cool the human body through perspiration. Entirely different and unknown laws of thermodynamics would have to be in effect for there to be no possibility of storms.

Volcanoes

Dead planets do not have volcanoes. Planet earth is far from dead—we live on a thin crust of solid material that surrounds a fiery ball of molten rock. Hot liquid rock below the surface of the earth, called magma, rises through buoyant forces, seeking to escape through the denser solid mantle surface. An incredible amount of potential energy (heat) is stored in the liquid rock and is sometimes violently released when a volcano erupts. When Mt. St. Helens erupted in 1980, it blew off a side of the mountain and sent one cubic kilometer of rock ash into the air. Mt. St. Helens is actually quite small when compared to the enormous eruption on the island of Krakatau in 1883. With a noise heard 4500 kilometers away, this volcano blew away two thirds of the island, and it launched 20 cubic kilometers of rock into the air. The violent shaking of the ocean floor generated massive tidal waves that killed 36,000 people and destroyed numerous seaside villages. To those who lived on a tropical island paradise in the path of these tsunamis, this volcano was anything but "very good."

According to the Perfect Paradise Paradigm, there could have been no volcanoes before the fall. Because volcanoes are a product of the basic laws of nature, either the governing laws of nature were different or the earth itself was considerably different. It therefore requires a great deal of imagination to explain what that world might have been like. Since the Scriptures are silent on this presumption, advocates of the Perfect Paradise Paradigm are free to imagine whatever they wish. Some suggest the earth was a solid mass of rock.[4] Others speculate that the surface of the earth was thicker. Some have even considered that there was no movement of crustal plates to generate stresses and fissures in the surface. Whatever the case is presumed to be, the planet imagined by the Perfect Paradise Paradigm is not at all like planet earth. It goes vastly beyond a clear reading of Scripture to find any indication that the curse or the flood brought about global changes of this magnitude.[5]

Nature by Design

Many other inconsistencies could be illustrated where the Perfect Paradise Paradigm imagines a world with different laws

---

[4] Nor would a solid planet necessarily be a better place. The circulating molten magma under the earth's crust is thought to be the source of our planet's magnetic field that serves to shield us from deadly solar radiation. Without a solid planet, there is no magnetic field, and the earth is not such a paradise after all.

[5] Neither does nature record changes of this nature. If energetic changes of this manner had occurred, the dynamic response of the planet would be clearly perceptible today. The absence of evidence indicates that the earth never underwent these changes imagined by the Perfect Paradise Paradigm. Otherwise, the evidence would have been hidden by the very Creator who speaks through nature to reveal His character.

of nature than are in operation today. Yet a more significant problem with the young earth creationism paradigm is that the Creator takes credit for creating the very things that are not permitted by that paradigm. The same laws of nature that young earth creationism claims would be contrary to His nature apart from sin are attested to by Scripture as the perfect design of God to accomplish His purpose and bring Him glory. Far from shying away from the power of nature, God uses the ferocity of nature to illustrate His sovereign power. The laws of nature in operation today are "very good" because they serve the Master's purpose.

Consider the Psalmist's reasons for praising the Creator:

"Praise the LORD!
Praise the LORD from the heavens;
Praise Him in the heights!
Praise Him, all His angels;
Praise Him, all His hosts!
Praise Him, sun and moon;
Praise Him, all stars of light!
Praise Him, highest heavens,
And the waters that are above the heavens!
Let them praise the name of the LORD,
For He commanded and they were created.
He has also established them forever and ever;
He has made a decree which will not pass away.

Praise the LORD from the earth,
Sea monsters and all deeps;
Fire and hail, snow and clouds;
Stormy wind, fulfilling His word;
Mountains and all hills;
Fruit trees and all cedars;
Beasts and all cattle;
Creeping things and winged fowl. (Psalm 148:1–10)

This Psalm speaks of all creation giving praise to God, including the sun, moon, stars, "sea monsters and all deeps, fire and hail, snow and clouds; stormy wind, fulfilling his word." As one commentator eloquently states, "God made the universe so that it would show forth the excellence of his character."[6] Thus the Bible explicitly states that God is exalted by violent natural processes and that they serve in "fulfilling His word"! These weather patterns are not inconsistent with His nature; indeed they fulfill His command. The Psalmist says that God uses the current weather patterns for His glory and according to His plan. Stormy weather is "very good" when used for God's purpose.

According to the Bible, the laws of nature that sometimes cause harm had a definite place in God's original creation. Of course the fall does not make it acceptable for God to do things that He could not or would not do otherwise. If a tornado was inherently evil, God could not use its stormy winds to fulfill His command. Clearly, the sin of man does not make it permissible for God to avail Himself of natural processes if they are otherwise inconsistent with His character. God can do no evil, and the things God does are right whether they are done before or after the fall of man.

All of these natural processes, then, were created before man walked the earth and have always given their Creator praise. The present laws of nature were created by God in the beginning for His purposes and did not change after the fall or the flood. The psalmist states that God has "established them forever and ever; He has made a decree which will not pass away." This is a biblical statement that the laws of nature have never changed. They are an immutable witness to His glory.

---

[6] Grudem, *Systematic Theology*, Zondervan, 1995, p. 159.

Pleasure and Pain

Physical pain was not part of the original creation according to the Perfect Paradise Paradigm. It is something that came about after the fall. But some things that bring pain and suffering also bring pleasure. Norman Geisler points out that "in a physical world where there is water for boating and swimming, some will drown. If there are mountains to climb, there must be valleys into which one may fall."[7] Pleasure and pain are sometimes opposite sides of the same coin. Pain in some instances is simply a more intense sensation of pleasure. We may not be able to have one without the other. A symphony can be music to the ears, but it can also bring on a migraine if the volume is too loud. To experience pleasure without pain requires more than divine sustenance, it requires a completely different set of natural laws.[8]

Physical pain is arguably a gift from God. Protection from injury and harm is often the purpose of physical pain. Even in Eden, Adam would have needed the sensations of pain to prevent injury while cultivating the garden or going about his daily business. There certainly is no biblical basis for assuming that Adam could not trip and fall, bump his head on a tree limb, scratch himself, or burn his hand in a fire.[9] Neither Satan nor Adam had

---

[7] Geisler, Norman L., *The Roots of Evil*, Zondervan, Grand Rapids MI, 1978, p. 72.

[8] Simply being able to describe this paradise does not mean that the reality must be logically possible. Perhaps there is no set of physical laws that would provide the physical sensation of pleasure without the sensation of pain as well. In heaven there will be pleasure without pain, but that sensation may be of a completely different type than could exist in this perishable physical world.

[9] Hugh Ross and others point out that there is actually positive proof in the Bible that pain existed in the "very good" world before the fall. When the curse was directed at Eve, God said, "I will greatly multiply your pain in childbirth" (Genesis 3:16). Because something multiplied by nothing equals nothing, to multiply her pain means that pain was already associated with childbirth before the fall.

to ask what "a bruised heel" was. Physical pain was not a foreign concept invented after the fall.

Accidents

One weekend while I was in college, my dad asked me to come home because a neighbor needed our help. One of the elderly farmer's pigs had slipped down an embankment and gotten stuck in a pond. After trying in vain to pull the huge pig out of the pond, we were left with only one option. The farmer's freezer was filled with pork a little sooner than he had planned. What would this have looked like if it had taken place in God's original creation?

The Perfect Paradise Paradigm is especially fuzzy on the "good/bad thing" when it comes to accidents. It is unclear as to what sorts of accidents were impossible prior to the fall and what sorts were hypothetically possible but providentially prevented. It is simply speculated that there were no accidents or injuries in the Perfect Paradise. According to that notion, wayward animals like my neighbor's pig would have been kept from sliding down slippery slopes. No animals would have ever gotten stuck in the mud or injured. Termite mounds would never be trampled by an elephant. A fly would never suffer when swatted by the tail of a cow. Of course the fly would have avoided the cow altogether because the nuisance to the cow wouldn't be "very good." To young earth creationism proponents, it is inconceivable that a ladybug sitting on the backside of a leaf would be caught up in brush eaten by a giraffe. After all, "death, bloodshed, and suffering of living creatures were not possible before the fall."[10]

Even though young earth creationism claims to be faithful to a clear reading of Scripture, this scenario is nothing more than an extreme and imaginative inference born out of sentimental specu-

---

[10] Ham, Ken, "Adam and the Ants," *Back To Genesis*, No. 33a, September, 1991, The Institute of Creation Research.

lation. God's Word does not say that divine providence directed the path of elephants, strategically located termite mounds off the beaten path, separated ladybugs from leaves at inopportune times, or kept animals away from slippery slopes. To assume that divine intervention was continuously required in this manner presses the Scriptures to the point of trivializing God's providence.

Moreover, a world that requires constant intervention to prevent the normal operation of its laws is not a "very good" creation in any sense of the word. If all of life was created so significantly ill-suited for the environment in which it lived that it took the intervention of God's power simply to sustain it, that world was not created good at all. Yet this internal inconsistency is multiplied countless times by those who claim that there was no animal death or suffering before the fall.

Hunger

Young earth creationism assumes that "there was, therefore, nothing bad in that created world, no hunger, no struggle for existence, no suffering, and certainly no death of animal or human life anywhere in God's perfect creation."[11] Since neither hunger nor fatigue was possible in the Perfect Paradise, everywhere and at all times there must have been an abundant supply of vegetation. It simply would not be "very good" for an animal to stray into a barren locale where it would feel the pangs of hunger. Hence, every species must have had a diet based on a universally available food supply. Moreover, the food supply had to be sufficiently abundant for the growing population of the countless species that were filling the earth.[12]

---

[11] Morris, Henry, "The Fall, The Curse, and Evolution," *Back To Genesis*, No. 112a, April 1998, The Institute of Creation Research.

[12] Dietary requirements and food sources could not have been dependent on a local environment because otherwise animals might move outside their ecological niche as they spread and filled the earth.

Another possibility is that there was no hunger because there was no need to eat. Instead of focusing on the supply side, the problem is solved by removing the demand. But in that case, why bother with eating at all? One might argue that a better design for life destined for immortality and perfection would not require eating. Perhaps eating in paradise might have merely been for pleasure—Eve did say that the forbidden fruit looked good and was tasty. Yet this shallow justification rings hollow as well.

Clearly food was provided in abundance to meet a real physical need, a need that would have been made apparent through hunger. Moreover, apart from the physical sensation of hunger, the temptation to eat from the tree would have been greatly lessened. The fact that Eve was tempted to satisfy her need outside the bounds of God's provision indicates that the potential for hunger was very real. The Creator's ample provision meant that the inhabitants of the garden would not hunger as long as man obeyed. But that in no way implies that hunger was not possible for any creature anywhere in the entire created world. To assume otherwise is to simply read between the lines of Scripture.

Reproduction

Perhaps the most distinct—although implicit—biblical support for animal death before the fall is the Creator's instruction for all living creatures to "be fruitful and multiply" (Genesis 1:22, 28). Reproduction was created for the express purpose of filling the earth, the sky, and the seas.

The typical assumption is that the animal population was to expand and populate the initially uninhabited earth. This is a curious instruction if there was no animal death. If animals were immortal and multiplied as instructed, at some point the animals would fill the earth. Would God have issued a stop order? Was God's plan to remove the reproductive abilities of the immortal animals and fundamentally alter their instincts? Of course the assumption that animals would have ceased reproducing at some point is conjecture. The animals were instructed to be fruitful and multiply with no qualifications or timetable. Indeed, the Scripture clearly states that the Creator would not fundamentally alter the biology or behavior of the entire animal kingdom after the earth was full because God ceased creating after the sixth day. If the goal had been to fill the earth with immortal animals, God could have simply created an initial population large enough to fill the earth and be done with it.[13]

Reproduction originally had the same purpose it has today. Reproduction was the Creator's means of sustaining the species after the death of previous generations. By being fruitful and multiplying, the animals were not to merely grow in number and disperse, but more importantly they were to perpetuate the species.

Animal death before the fall is also indicated by the phrase "fill the earth." Interestingly the King James translates the instruction as "replenish the earth," which carries the clear connotation of replacement. Similarly, "fill" may also be interpreted as "refresh," in which case the association between reproduction and animal death is clear and explicit. Much like the unending cycles of seasons, reproduction serves the purpose of refreshing and replenishing species as succeeding generations pass.[14]

Filling the earth indicates that the Creator did not create an unchanging immortal world. He fashioned a dynamic ecosystem, one that changed with time. Here in the beginning, in the dynamic, temporal state of nature is evidence that the plan of God on earth was unfolding with time. This was not the eternal abode of man and beast—it was created to serve a purpose in time.

---

[13] In fact, since the Perfect Paradise Paradigm equates speed of creation with power of God, immediately filling the earth would have been more impressive and hence more perfect and "very good."

[14] Proverbs 3:10 uses the same verb as Genesis 1:28 in this sense.

Problems with the Perfect Paradise

Both creation camps agree that God has the power to do as He chooses. What separates the two views is not what God is able to do but what God actually did. To what extent did the Creator intervene in the normal affairs of His creation to prevent accidents before the fall? Did the Creator routinely disturb the laws of nature to intervene on behalf of His creatures? To what extent was the world so different that accidents and suffering were not even possible? For if the world was as described by the Perfect Paradise Paradigm, God either prevented all suffering or suffering was not even possible at all. The problem for the paradigm is that both options are contrary to the Word of God.

The Overworked "Sustaining Power" of God

"Miracle" is perhaps the most exhausted word in the English language. Everything from household cleaning products to over-the-counter drugs bears this overworked moniker. While no one would have predicted in the spring of 1969 that the New York Mets would win the World Series later that year, the "Miracle Mets" hardly compare to the creation of a universe out of nothing. But lest we reduce the fiat miracles of creation to the level of the 1969 Mets, we must be careful to not read miracle into the text when it is not intended.

The Genesis creation narrative is far from an exhaustive description of the life and times of Adam in the garden. The sparsity of Scripture poses a considerable challenge to the Perfect Paradise Paradigm. When pressed beyond metaphorical science and vague generalities of life in paradise, young earth creationism plugs the gaping holes in their idyllic worldview by creating an irrefutable principle. Whenever the imagined paradise is challenged, the response is to invoke the "sustaining power" of God.[15]

---

[15] See Deuteronomy 8:4. It is interesting that the context of this passage invalidates the applicability of this point to the creation week. The previous

Ham and Sarfati invented this general-purpose principle to describe a unique event in the history of Israel: "The Israelites wandered in the desert for 40 years, and yet their clothes didn't wear out, their shoes didn't wear out, and their feet didn't swell. Obviously God miraculously upheld their clothing, shoes, and feet so that they would not wear out or fall apart as the rest of creation is doing. One can only imagine what the world would be like if God upheld every detail of it like this." [16]

"Imagine" is exactly what must be done. The Scripture in no way suggests that God's specific means of provision for the Israelites during the exodus is a general principle that broadly applied to all of creation before the fall. Referring to Deuteronomy 8:4, Ham and Sarfati point out that God providentially preserved the clothes and shoes of the Israelites during the forty years they wandered in the desert. But the context of this passage invalidates the generalization of the principle to describe the world before the fall. His sustaining power was very specific in application.

During the Exodus, God was humbling His people to prove their faith and teach them to trust Him. He made them hungry, yet He provided them with manna. He made them wander countless miles through the harsh desert, but He kept their feet from swelling and their clothes from aging. God brought them to suffer in order to show His providential care. He was taking them to the Promised Land where they would rejoice in His bounty and trust His provision as they recalled His faithfulness during their time of need.

---

verses describe how God was testing His people in the desert, humbling them by letting them become hungry. The sustaining power of God was limited in application. Even in the context of God's sustaining power, suffering was brought on by His plan.

[16] Ham and Sarfati, *"Why is there Death and Suffering?"* Answers In Genesis, 2001, pp. 14,15.

This was clearly not like a Perfect Paradise before the fall. God's purpose was not to prevent the suffering of Israel but to use their suffering to prove His glory. He allowed them to suffer for a time to teach them His glory on the way to a better place. He had a purpose for the sufferings of His people that would lead to His own glory. Rather than justifying the Perfect Paradise Paradigm, this biblical example demonstrates the perspective of the Perfect Purpose Paradigm.

To what extent then did God intervene with His sustaining power to prevent suffering before the fall? The Bible gives absolutely no indication that God intervened in the affairs of His creation with sustaining power before the fall of man. The Bible teaches that God created the world through fiat miracle and upheld it through normal providence with minimal intervention. Genesis does not describe a world sustained by the routine intervention of the Creator. The Hebrew word for a distinctively divine act of creation, *bara*, is only used three times in the first chapter of Genesis. Normal process is seen working along with divine action as man is instructed to subdue, cultivate, eat, and reproduce (Genesis 1:28–29; 2:15). God used normal processes to plant trees in the garden and cause them to grow (Genesis 2:8–9). There simply is no indication that the Creator's sustaining power was needed to uphold or maintain the "very good" creation. To extrapolate the principle of sustaining power to become the norm before the fall exploits the silence of the Scriptures and presses the miraculous to a trivial extreme.

Ironically, the principle of God's sustaining power contradicts the spirit of the Perfect Paradise Paradigm. To sustain means to maintain a state, keep from falling or failing, or supply what is needed to survive. The shoes of the Israelites needed to be sustained because otherwise they would wear out. But in a Perfect Paradise, the created order and laws of nature would not have had to be constantly violated to maintain their goodness. Nothing wore out in that idyllic paradise. A need for continual upholding would only indicate a deficiency in the very fabric of that "very good" creation. The very need for sustaining power proves that the Perfect Paradise Paradigm is internally inconsistent.

Cause and Effect

Young earth creationism asserts that God involved Himself in creation to prevent suffering and accidents before the fall. While God is certainly able to interrupt the affairs of His creation to prevent suffering and difficulties, He is not willing to interfere to that extreme. If God were to routinely preempt the natural processes of our world, there would be no principle of cause and effect and there would be no foundation for rational thought. Rational thought depends entirely on the dependable relationship between causes and their effects, to the degree that a world without causality is a world without free will.

> Thus, in a world which operates according to divine miraculous intervention, there would be no necessary relation between phenomena, and in particular between cause and effect. In some instances one event would follow from a certain set of conditions, another time a different event, and so on, such that ultimately an uncountable variety of events would follow a given set of conditions. There would be no regularity of consequence, no natural production of effects. . . . Hence we could not know or even suppose what course of action to take to accomplish a certain rationally conceived goal. Thus, we could neither propose action nor act ourselves.[17]

It simply would not be benevolent of God to create rational beings and then confuse and frustrate them through routine in-

---

[17] Reichenbach, Bruce, "Natural Evils and Natural Laws: A Theodicy for Natural Evils," *International Philosophical Quarterly,* Vol. 16, 1976, p. 187.

terventions to prevent the consequences of their actions. Clearly, this is not a better world. Yet this is exactly the type of world envisioned by the Perfect Paradise Paradigm.

The chaos resulting from the Creator's continual miraculous intervention would also invalidate our moral accountability to the Creator. In fact, to argue that God would routinely pre-empt His natural order is to mock God. Recall the warning of Paul in Galatians 6:7; "Do not be deceived, God is not mocked; for whatever a man sows, this he will also reap." In this principle of the harvest is an implicit endorsement of the law of causality. God will indeed bring about the consequences of our decisions and actions. To assume otherwise is to mock God.

Even though it is difficult, it is exactly because I love my children deeply that I must let them occasionally suffer the consequences of their decisions. Children simply do not learn responsibility when their parents continually intervene for their protection. Our heavenly Father knows and practices this principle as well. From the beginning the Creator taught humanity that actions bring consequences. This principle of the harvest applies equally to Adam as it does today. Had God routinely pre-empted the natural order He created, Adam would not have learned responsibility and accountability from observing the world around him. Had causality been impeded prior to the fall, Adam would have no reason to appreciate the consequences of his actions. He would not respect the fact that he was morally accountable to God and would reap what he sowed.

This mockery of God is the basis for Satan's lie to Eve. He deceived her into thinking that her actions would not bring the forewarned consequences. His lie would have been credible if there were no principal of cause and effect. Absent causality, it would not be unusual for an act to bring about many different results, none of which were harmful or unseemly in their experience. Moreover, if divine miraculous intervention were the norm, why would God not intervene to prevent Adam from eating the fruit just as He routinely intervened to prevent other things that were "not good?" If routine intervention to prevent suffering and evil were the norm, then God would have certainly prevented evil by that most significant divine intervention. But by virtue of God's character, divine intervention to prevent untoward consequences of harmful actions has never been the norm.

Focal Points

Clearly God has the power to do as He wishes. The Creator most certainly could have created a world without suffering or death if that had been His plan. Our eternal home with Christ will be such a place. But the Scripture explicitly tells us that future paradise will not be like this world. In sharp contrast, the imagination—and the Scriptures—must be stretched past their breaking point to arrive at the idyllic world of the Perfect Paradise Paradigm. A world where plants become poisonous, animals develop a taste for meat and the physiology to kill, and the entire plant and animal kingdoms evolve into completely different species and ecosystems is nothing more than mere conjecture.

Even the most ardent advocates of a young earth admit that the world of the Perfect Paradise Paradigm is not the clear teaching of the Bible. Henry Morris says that "the foregoing sequences of events *seem to be reasonably implied* by the Scriptural descriptions of the primeval world, the curse, the Flood, and the effects associated with each. However, *much is uncertain* and there is room for considerable research, both in Scripture and science, as to the details."[18] Far from a clear reading of Scripture, much of the young earth creationism worldview is speculation at best.

---

[18] Morris, Henry, *The Bible Has the Answers*, Master Books, 1987. Italics added.

In light of the innumerable uncertainties that form the foundation of the young earth creationism worldview, it is difficult to justify their claims of orthodoxy. This reliance on implications from the presumption of paradise indicates that questioning this worldview is not a compromise of biblical authority. Although it is the standard teaching in many churches today, thinking believers who love God with all of their minds will recognize the peril of paradise.

FITNESS AND THE FALL

Recently I had the privilege of taking a cruise in one of Alaska's glacier-carved fjords. Otters playfully floated on their backs, and sea lions barked from rocky outcroppings as our boat made its way through the icy waters. The eagerly anticipated highlight of the day came when a pod of humpback whales surfaced in the distance.

Humpbacks are beautiful creatures with an elegance and power that is awesome to observe. While we were waiting for the whales to surface, the captain instructed us to be very quiet so as not to disturb the animals. In fact, boats intentionally keep a considerable distance from the whales because encroachment by curious humans can disturb their environment. Since it is up to the whales to show themselves, it's rare that humans get to see the whales up close.

Like the endangered humpback whale, many species depend on habitats that must be protected from slight changes that might otherwise lead to their demise. Often, we go to great lengths to protect the habitats of endangered species only to learn all too often just how fragile their environments are. While it is readily apparent that animals are highly fit and well designed for their particular environments, many species are not very tolerant to changes in their habitat. Their survival depends on specific food sources, climate, geography, and even interaction with other species in their particular ecological niche.

Design in nature is a compelling argument for the Creator's existence. Fitness in nature, however, leads to an inextricable contradiction when the "very good" creation is defined as perfect in every way.

Not Perfect for Paradise

According to leaders of the young earth creationism movement, "There was, therefore, nothing bad in that created world, no hunger, no struggle for existence, no suffering, and certainly no death of animal or human life in God's perfect creation."[1] The foundational premise is that if the animals were declared "very good," they must have been perfectly suited for the Perfect Paradise. The problem is that many species alive today are especially well suited to present-day ecologies but would have been unfit for that Perfect Paradise. Many of our current species simply could not survive (and certainly not thrive) in that Perfect Paradise. Something must have happened to change the perfect species' in the Perfect Paradise to enable them to survive after the fall. Exactly what is a serious problem and an open question for the paradigm of young earth creationism.

Young earth creationism leaders dismiss this conundrum by first minimizing the change that took place and then by inventing new laws of genetics to engineer the massive changes. When one recognizes the immense changes that must have taken place, their language of "minor adaptations" becomes utterly irrelevant. Young earth creationism scientists then have the same problem

---

[1] Morris, Henry, "The Fall, the Curse, and Evolution," *Back To Genesis,* No. 112a, April 1998.

as Neo-Darwinian evolutionists—they must explain how life that exists today came about from what it was before.

Symbiotic Relationships

Nile crocodiles are fearful predators with a soft spot in their heart for the Egyptian plover. Together they provide a good example of a mutually beneficial, or symbiotic, relationship that is counter to their normal behavior. In a phenomenon known as "cleaning symbiosis," the plover feeds on parasites while perched in the open mouth of the crocodile. The crocodile instinctively knows it is better to get its teeth cleaned than to eat the bird. After the job is done, the bird will hop out of the crocodile's mouth and make a clean getaway.

Darwinian evolution does not provide a compelling explanation for how this symbiosis evolved. One wonders how many plovers must have sacrificed their lives eating parasites before the crocodile learned it was best to let the bird escape. It must have taken a lot of bravery, or hunger, or lucky stupidity for the birds to try this maneuver even though they witnessed other feathery friends getting eaten by crocodiles. A much better solution to this mystery of origin is that the Creator explicitly designed the behavior of the Nile crocodiles and Egyptian plovers for their mutual benefit and His glory.

Although problematic for naturalistic evolution, this mutualism is an even greater problem for the Perfect Paradise Paradigm. Cleaning symbiosis benefits the Nile crocodile by removing parasites and preventing tooth decay. Likewise it benefits the bird by providing nourishment. But in the "very good" world of the Perfect Paradise Paradigm, there was no hunger. There were no parasites. Nor was there any tooth decay or the need for cleaning teeth.

Clearly there would have been no cleaning symbiosis in the Perfect Paradise. Every bird would be safe in a Perfect Paradise where crocodiles do not eat birds. In fact, if there were no hunger and no death by starvation, there would be no need for the birds to eat parasites. Nor would the crocodiles need to eat the birds. There would be no need to eat at all. And if the birds and crocodiles did actually need to eat, there would be an abundant supply of plant food. Only after the fall would the plover begin eating crocodile parasites and the Nile crocodile begin eating birds. How this mutualism arose after the fall is a problem that must be answered by the Perfect Paradise Paradigm.

Defense Mechanisms

Defense mechanisms demonstrate a high degree of design from an intelligent Creator. One of the better examples of this is the bombardier beetle. "Bomby" is a favorite amongst young earth creationism teachers because it strongly demonstrates intelligent design and presents a challenge for naturalistic evolution.

The bombardier beetle gets its name from the ability to fire a mixture of boiling-hot toxic chemicals from its posterior. Chemicals secreted by the beetle are collected in a reservoir and released through a muscle-controlled valve into a reaction chamber. Chemical reactions generate enough heat to bring the toxins to the boiling point and the increased pressure forces the mixture out of beetle in a lethal stream. This ability serves the beetle to protect it from would-be danger.

Yet many who use Bomby to argue for design in creation fail to recognize the inherent contradiction with their creation paradigm. This attribute of design is meaningful only in the context of a need for defense. There can be no benign function served by this capability. Only in a world with predators and prey does the bombardier beetle appear intelligently designed. Moreover, bombardier beetles are predators themselves. If a beetle did not have a functional defense mechanism and survived on a herbivorous diet before the fall, that would be an entirely distinct species from the bombardier beetle alive today. The inescapable conclusion is that there were no bombardier beetles in the "very good" world envisioned by the Perfect Paradise Paradigm.

Another interesting counterexample to the Perfect Paradise Paradigm is when an otherwise defenseless species will leverage the defense mechanism of another species to its own advantage. Goby fish are relatively defenseless in themselves, but the Creator has provided for their protection in an interesting way. These fish are known to live within the toxic spines of a sea urchin to gain protection from predators. What is lethal to other intruders is a safe harbor for the Goby fish. Clownfish gain similar protection from predators through symbiosis with anemones. Examples abound in nature where a symbiotic relationship benefits the survival of one or both species in a manner that would be completely unnecessary or counterproductive in a Perfect Paradise.

All of this begs the question how and when the complex interdependencies and defense mechanisms arose. Why would the Creator design defensive mechanisms into perfect species when there was nothing to defend against? If there were no need for defense in the Perfect Paradise, then the sea urchin would not need toxic spines. Nor would the occasion for symbiotic relationships arise in a Perfect Paradise. Moreover, lethal streams of hot gas and poisonous spines could not exist in a perfect world with no chance of harm or death. Like most species alive today, sea urchins and bombardier beetles could not have existed in the Perfect Paradise.

Dietary Designs

Young earth creationism asserts that all animals were herbivores until the degenerative effects of man's sin made some of them into carnivores (the biblical basis for this supposition will be examined in a later chapter). In an attempt to minimize the significance of this change, young earth creationism leaders argue that, "since many animals with sharp teeth and claws were designed to eat plants, it was only behavior, not anatomy, that changed after

Eden."[2] This statement is both logically fallacious and factually incorrect. A few examples are not necessarily representative of all cases. Simply because a few species of herbivores were designed with sharp teeth and claws does not mean that all animals with sharp teeth and claws were originally designed to be herbivores. More important, the notion that herbivores could degenerate into carnivores is false. Carnivorous digestive systems are fundamentally distinct from herbivore systems. The mouth of a typical carnivore contains incisors, canines, and molar teeth set in both jaws whereas a typical herbivore has flat molars set in both jaws and incisors only in the lower jaw. The jaws of a carnivore move up and down to tear and crush food while the jaws of an herbivore move in a circular motion to grind food. Furthermore, herbivores are able to digest the cellulose that forms the cell walls of plants while carnivores are not.

The stomach of a carnivore is also much smaller than the chambered stomach of a ruminant herbivore. Even though a carnivore's high metabolic rate requires a prodigious caloric intake, the higher fat and calorie content of meat enables a carnivore to subsist on one small meal per day. In sharp contrast, the relatively slower metabolism of an herbivore requires fewer calories, but due to the low caloric content of vegetation, an herbivore eats virtually continuously by consuming the food stored in its large stomach. Carnivores can survive without a stomach, colon, or cecum. Herbivores cannot. Carnivores can survive without microorganisms. Herbivores cannot. Carnivores can survive without plant food. Herbivores cannot. The digestive efficiency of herbivores is only about 50 percent while for carnivores it is almost 100 percent. Differences between species also include distinctly different enzymes, bacteria, and micro-organisms operating in the digestive system to process nutrients from meat and various plant

---

[2] Morris, Henry III, *After Eden*, Master Books, 2003, p. 117.

tissues. The entire anatomy, physiology, and biochemical makeup of carnivores is designed for eating meat.

Young earth creationism proponents admit that this is a serious challenge to their creation paradigm.

> One should also not overlook the full extent of what is involved in any particular defense-attack mechanism. For instance, discussions on the shape of teeth and claws may overlook the fact that the design features for meat-eating in the great cats are much more than just sharp teeth. A lion has finely-programmed hunting instincts, and immense muscular power capable of breaking a wildebeest's neck with one blow. Its digestive system is attuned to a diet of fresh meat (though lions can cope with vegetables in a crisis and, since meat is easier to digest, degenerative changes could be responsible for dependence on meat). All this makes it overwhelmingly appear to be a highly designed hunting and killing machine.[3]

Quite clearly, the carnivores that have existed since the fall are fundamentally different animals than those creatures that are suggested to have existed in the Perfect Paradise.

Even if "lions can cope with vegetables in a crisis," that does not sound "very good." Should life in a Perfect Paradise before the fall be described as a "crisis?" If the animals were created "very good" as defined by that paradigm, the pre-fall animal kingdom would certainly have been optimized for an herbivorous diet. The carnivores of today would by no means be fit for the world of the Perfect Paradise Paradigm.

---

[3] Batten, Donald, editor, *The Revised & Expanded Answers Book*, Creation Science Foundation, 1990.

Extreme Habitats

The Perfect Paradise Paradigm imagines a world before the fall with uniformly hospitable habitats around the globe. Yet the world today is anything but uniformly hospitable. Species today thrive on distinctly different habitats and many would suffer or die if they were placed into a substantially different environment. For example, Polar bears are designed for habitats that would kill desert animals. Likewise, there would presumably be no home for the desert cactus in the Perfect Paradise. Whatever is imagined as the hospitable global climate of the Perfect Paradise would ultimately be inhospitable for numerous species alive today. That simply does not seem "very good."

An even more significant problem is one of co-adaptation. It is not simply that individual species are adapted to an environment; multiple species of plants and animals are mutually adapted to each other in a very complex and integrated fashion. If environmental changes at the fall or the flood brought about the relatively immediate[4] emergence of modern species, then each individual species in a coupled ecosystem would have to simultaneously adapt to each other in a dynamic fashion. As one species adapted to changes in the dynamic ecosystem, it would require simultaneous re-adaptation of all other mutually dependent species. And in turn, each mutually dependent species would have to re-adapt to each cycle of re-adaptation. This rapid tail-wagging-the-dog phenomenon would spiral into the destruction of the ecosystem rather than rapidly converging to an optimally balanced, delicate, and complex interdependent ecosystem.

---

[4] The supposed emergence of modern species must have happened over the span of years or hundreds of years which is a mere blink of the eye for the levels of biological change inferred by young earth creationists.

Immune Systems

Immune systems are another example of an entire biological system that would have no purpose if there were nothing harmful to defend against. These sophisticated systems demand considerable overhead on the body in terms of taxing energy and other physiological resources. To suggest that they would have been present in animal life before the fall seems to contradict the Perfect Paradise of Eden. If they were indeed absent before the fall, their ubiquitous presence today not only demands a totally new creation after the fall, it also superbly evidences design in nature.

Bad Designs for a Very Good World

The problem with the Perfect Paradise Paradigm is not trivial. By definition, a Perfect Paradise would demand more than simply the ability to survive. If the animals were perfect before the fall, one would expect optimal fitness and adaptation for that perfect environment. But the animal kingdom of today is remarkably well designed for the present day ecosystems and not a Perfect Paradise. Proponents of the Perfect Paradise Paradigm must therefore explain how and when the changes came about that resulted in the well-designed animals and plants alive today. Unfortunately, such answers expose the fallacy of the Perfect Paradise Paradigm.

One common response is that the Creator anticipated the demands of the post-fall world, "so He created animals with features they would need in the new economy. Or it may be that these features had some other more benign function originally."[5] Animals would have been created with sharp teeth, powerful loins and jaws, lightning-fast speed, toxic spines, and explosive chemical reservoirs, yet such attributes served some unknown and hypo-

---

[5] Morris, John D., "If All Animals were Created as Plant Eaters, Why Do Some Have Sharp Teeth?" *Back To Genesis*, No. 100b, April 1997.

thetical purpose in the Perfect Paradise. In this way, the Creator initially fashioned His creatures without harmful attributes. These benign features then took on a new and more ominous function after the fall.

A similar explanation is that animals were designed with functions that would only become operative when needed after the fall. These latent traits would not be functional before the fall since they would serve no purpose. Perhaps the term "reverse vestigiality" best describes these useless attributes designed into a species in anticipation of their fitness for the post-fall world.[6]

At first glance, this seems like a reasonable answer. The Creator had the foreknowledge to see what His creation would need, and He created species with the means to survive after the fall. But the dragon is not slain so easily. Whether the design features were initially latent or served some other purpose, this approach fails on several points.

When the incalculable number of examples of traits that are inconsistent with a Perfect Paradise are considered, it strains credulity to assume that all these features would have been latent or benign before the fall. It simply stretches the imagination to suppose that every feature that makes a species fit after the fall could have been inoperative or have had a benign function in Paradise. By their very design, defense mechanisms are far from benign. Toxic spines and snake venom are far from inoperative and cannot have a benign function.

It is important to understand that a species cannot be simultaneously optimized for multiple environments. Optimality in nature is not so general. A feature designed to render fitness after the fall would render the species much less than perfect for the

---

[6] A vestigial structure in a biological system is one which has no present use and is assumed to be an evolutionary artifact. In that sense, a reverse vestigial function would be one that does not yet have a need but will after the organism changes.

Perfect Paradise. Therefore to assert that animals and plants were created with latent or benign capabilities in the Perfect Paradise is much more than mere speculation, it is wild imagination that is not based on the record of nature or a clear reading of Scripture.

Ironically, delayed functionality is a direct accommodation of God's awareness of the coming fall into the original creation. Implicit in this view is the assumption that God created life in the Perfect Paradise with more than just the garden in mind. This view then is in agreement with the theme of the Perfect Purpose Paradigm.

Re-Designed for a Not-So-Good World

Since latent or benign capabilities do not solve the quandary, then the only option left for the young earth creationism worldview is a complete transformation of the entire animal and plant kingdoms after the fall. Truly the plant and animal species before the fall would have had to be substantially altered to the degree that they would become entirely new species after the fall.

Two options are proposed by the Perfect Paradise Paradigm for what brought about this transformation of species: either the species were changed by an external source or they possessed the innate potential for radical and abrupt modification within themselves. Both options conflict with the clear teaching of Scripture, sound science, and the record of nature.

Re-Created Species

Young earth creationism enlists the science of genetics to substantiate the generation of new species when they suggest that, "each of these changes requires a DNA alteration."[7] Appealing to an external cause, some young earth creationists suggest that Satan altered the genes of species throughout the

---

[7] Morris, John D.,ibid.

entire creation: "Is it possible that this highly intelligent being performed breeding experiments, or genetic engineering on both mankind (Genesis 6:2–4 perhaps) and the animals, in his attempt to mock the true Creator-God and usurp His authority? Perhaps even the ancient legends of composite mixtures of beasts and half men/half beast have some basis in fact."[8] Aside from the appeal to fantasy and legend in order to substantiate a distinction between life today and that before the fall, this speculation errs by attributing creative ability to Satan.

More serious than just inviting ridicule, speculating that Satan modified living creatures after the fall contradicts sound theology. Satan has been given considerable authority, but not the ability to create new species. The Scriptures teach that all things that have come into being have come into being through God alone (Colossians 1:16; John 1:3). To attribute the responsibility to Satan for essentially recreating the entire animal kingdom is akin to attributing the work of God to Satan. One could also question why the creation would bear such strong evidence of the Creator's glory in the design of nature if the Adversary had done it.

For this reason, most young earth creationists prefer to think that it was God who tinkered with the gene pool. Essentially, the Creator would have completely redesigned all animal and plant life after the fall through a genetic re-creation. The language of the curse does not indicate anything of this scope, however. Just as the Perfect Paradise Paradigm reads between the lines of the creation narrative to broadly apply the "sustaining power of God," it reads between the lines of the curse and extends its reach to radically transform the entire animal and plant kingdoms at the genetic level. All of this eisegesis[9] is motivated by a sentimental view of what God must have meant when He said creation was "very good."

---

[8] Ibid.

[9] Eisegesis is reading into the words of Scripture based on a paradigm rather than exegesis which is reading from the text in an expository fashion.

Not only does the Bible not teach this effect of the curse, this speculation directly violates the Scriptures. Genetic modification of this magnitude is nothing less than the creation of entirely new species. The creation of new species after the fall cannot be attributed to God because the Scriptures plainly state that God rested from creating after the sixth day. The notion that either Satan or God re-created various species after the fall is, simply put, false theology.

A Bottomless Gene Pool

Understanding that the Bible disallows the speculation that the animal and plant kingdoms were re-created after the fall by either God or Satan, the only option remaining for the Perfect Paradise Paradigm is that a vast and systemic change to virtually the entire plant and animal kingdoms occurred rapidly and naturally. In other words, the curse and the flood brought about such significant environmental changes that it forced the animals to rapidly adapt or die.

Young earth creationism scientists explain this wholesale change by claiming that, "a great deal more potential for variation was placed in the original genome."[10] Anticipating the changes that would come, God supposedly programmed excess information in the gene pool of each "kind" to enable gross variability after the fall and the flood. After these species spread out, became isolated, and inbred, the genetic information was somehow depleted and the genomes of modern species were fixed. Interestingly these species that so adroitly adapted to the post-flood environments subsequently became fragile and vulnerable to extinction.

There are significant problems with this proposed solution to the Perfect Paradise conundrum. The most glaring problem is

---

[10] Ibid.

the magnitude and abruptness of the supposed enormous burst of speciation. Adaptation cannot begin to describe the immense changes that would have had to take place. While genetics and ecology can account for considerable variability within species, a copious gene pool simply cannot account for what would be in actuality the origination of substantially new species. Genetic variability of that magnitude vastly exceeds the bounds imposed by the Creator to ensure survival of the species. Such responsive adaptability within the original genomes would not lead to stable species but would rather spiral out of control into a potpourri of stillborn species or localized mutants.

Furthermore, young earth creationism scientists have only vague generalizations to describe how this hyper-speciation might have stopped. It is asserted that animals and plants somehow lost genetic information and the species became fixed by way of a natural process. No one is able to explain what caused this hypothetical genetic information to be lost or even what it means to lose excess genetic information.

Like a pair of broken bookends, this solution has problems with the beginning and the end. How the speciation started and stopped is anyone's guess.

A fundamental misunderstanding of natural selection lies at the heart of this contention.[11] Natural selection works to preserve the fittest species during environmental changes. As such, natural selection is a stabilizing influence on an ecosystem. Natural selection does not produce changes in species—it removes the least fit and preserves the fittest species within an ecosystem. This critical point is missed by the young earth apologists: an organism must

---

[11] Natural selection should not be confused with naturalistic evolution. Natural selection is an observed principle of nature that simply means the most-fit species tend to survive and reproduce, hence increasing the presence of the fittest genome in the gene pool.

manifest a biological change before its fitness can be determined for selection and reproduction (e.g. it must develop an eye before the benefit of sight can be conferred and passed to succeeding generations). The mere presence of genetic information is of no selective value until it affects a change on the organism. Hence young earth creationism science must invent some unknown mechanism to actualize the hypothesized available genetic information to produce new traits *before* those new traits can be selected and preserved as a new species.[12] This point has yet to be addressed.

One can only wonder how the excessively rich gene pool generated entirely new plant and animal species immediately after the flood, but shortly thereafter the species became fixed, vulnerable to change, and susceptible to extinction. Why the genetic information was lost and how the species became fixed after the explosive post-fall speciation is answered by silence. This scenario cannot be deemed scientific because it is neither observable nor verifiable. The sudden loss of genetic information is only justified by its absence in today's species. This solution is sheer speculation built upon the gaps in scientific data and the silence of Scripture. It is an imaginary solution to account for how benign animals in an idyllic paradise became the diverse species alive today.

Hyper-Evolution

Hidden beneath the veneer of this argument from genetics is an appeal to theistic evolution.[13] The total systemic change of

---

[12] Evolutionists assert that mutations generate the changes to be operated upon by natural selection.

[13] Young earth creationists circumvent the association with evolution by inventing the distinction that this process of macro scale change is not evolutionary since it involves a loss of information rather than an increase of information. This parsing of terminology does not change the fact that their explanation amounts to an almost instantaneous and natural emergence of new species as environmental changes operate on the gene pool.

all plant and animal species due to genetic variability driven by environmental change is nothing other than an unimaginably rapid form of natural evolution. So rapid is the implied rate of evolutionary change that it vastly exceeds even the wildest scientific theories of evolution and defies the limits to biological change imposed by the Creator Himself. To attribute this modification of species to the work of God is nothing more than theistic hyper-evolution, that is, theistic evolution of a sort that no theistic evolutionist has ever proposed.

While young earth creationism scientists might balk at the suggestion that this view amounts to theistic evolution, it is undeniable. Using slightly different terminology, Henry Morris suggests that this latent tendency toward adaptation encoded in the animals amounted to God using genetic engineering: "Even animals that are now carnivores were originally herbivores. . . . The sharp teeth and other structures that are now used in eating flesh seem to be 'horizontal' variants, or mutants, of structures originally used in gnawing bark, tough roots, and the like. It may even be that God accomplished genetic engineering on the animals to forever remind Adam and Eve of the awful consequences of sin."[14] The term "mutants" is clearly an inference hyper-evolution.

Having exhausted all other alternatives to explain how paradise became perilous, young earth creationism must abandon Scripture and science and rely on wild speculation. The problem with this speculation is that the Perfect Paradise Paradigm violates the truth of God revealed in His word and in His creation. Neither direct, divine re-creation nor theistic hyper-evolution is an acceptable alternative. One is left to conclude that the Perfect

---

[14] Morris, Henry, "Adam and the Animals," Impact Article No. 212, The Institute for Creation Research, February 1991.

Paradise Paradigm does not offer a consistent and credible creation doctrine.

Focal Points

Speculating about what happened after the fall, Ken Ham notes, "Maybe some animals started eating each other."[15] This simplistic suggestion is no solution to a serious problem with the paradigm. Some animals did not just start eating others. More than mere behavior was involved. Nothing less than total systemic change would be required for animals perfectly created as plant eaters to become highly adapted carnivores after the fall. Even though some creationists simplistically imagine that somehow a lion developed a taste for meat, more than just the taste would have to change if it were originally a perfect plant eater. Along with the physiological changes of digestion, teeth structure, and musculature would come new instinctive behavior as well. Moreover, entire ecosystems would have had to change in concert to ensure the survival of the changing species. These coordinated changes would have had to take place rapidly in order to ensure the survival of changing species in a rapidly changing ecosystem. As we have seen, the various speculations as to the means by which such radical changes could have come about are unconvincing.

Simply put, animals designed for the world of today would not thrive, and many could not survive in the perfection of the paradise envisioned by young earth creationism. Exactly how life went from what it was then to what it is now is left open to speculation. "Whether such structures as fangs and claws were part of the original equipment, or were recessive features which only became dominant due to selection processes later, or were mu-

---

[15] Ham, Ken, "What Really Happened to the Dinosaurs," Answers in Genesis, 2001, p. 24.

tational features following the curse, or exactly what, must await further research."[16] In other words, what happened is anyone's guess. Unfortunately for the young earth creationism paradigm, those guesses all lead to dead ends.

When taken to the logical extreme, the Perfect Paradise Paradigm either demands theistic hyper-evolution or a compromise of clear biblical teaching. Each of these potential solutions falls short of resolving the conflict between fitness and the Perfect Paradise Paradigm. Young earth creationism ultimately must fall back to their foundational premise: it had to be so because it was "very good." This is neither good science nor good theology.

---

[16] Morris, Henry, *The Genesis Record*, p. 78.

PART 4

SUFFERING, DEATH, AND THE FALL

SUFFERING AND THE PLAN OF GOD

September 11, 2001, is a date indelibly imprinted on the memory of our nation. It was on that date that evil and death confronted America in a way that it had never experienced before. With live television coverage the nation stood by and watched in horror as innocent lives and icons of the American society were destroyed. As the death toll reached the thousands, it became clear that this was an act motivated by hatred and evil. Many Christians were asking how God could have allowed this to happen.

Crises like 9/11 bring us face to face with troubling questions: Could God have stopped these tragedies? Did He not know they were going to happen? If God is good and powerful, why is there so much evil and suffering in the world?

Yet this atrocity is not unique. Suffering and death have been a part of the fabric of human existence since the first couple inhabited a garden paradise. Throughout history people have struggled to reconcile the reality of suffering with the existence of a loving and all-powerful God. Many reject the Christian faith because they simply cannot reconcile the issue. Skeptics have every right to ask how evil and suffering came about. Why the Creator allows evil to persist is an even more urgent question.

As Christians living in a world with evil and suffering, we must be prepared to give a reason for the hope within us, a hope based on faith in a loving, wise, merciful, and all-powerful Creator.

It is important to understand that the Bible does not avoid this difficult issue. Quite the contrary. The Scriptures present a consistent worldview that affirms not only the goodness of the Creator but also the existence of evil and suffering in His creation. To properly reconcile the existence of evil and suffering with a loving and all-powerful God, one must consider the Master's purpose for the world He created.

The Problem of Evil

On February 12, 1809, two men were born that would forever change their world. Believing that God had created all men equally, Abraham Lincoln changed the way Americans regard their fellow man. Believing that all men evolved without God, Charles Darwin changed the way men regard their Creator.

Darwin began his voyage on the HMS Beagle as a twenty-two year old who believed the Bible's story of creation. Five years and forty thousand miles later, Darwin was well on his way to becoming convinced of a naturalistic evolution of life. His observations and speculations would eventually be published in the revolutionary book, *The Origin of Species*.

Perhaps surprisingly, Darwin was motivated more by theology than theory. He was confounded by the suffering and death he so frequently observed in nature. He could not believe that a loving Creator would allow such suffering. "There seems to me to be too much misery in the world," he wrote to his friend Asa Gray, the American preacher and botanist. "I cannot persuade myself that a beneficent and omnipotent God would have designedly created the ichneumonidae (a parasite) with the express intention of their feeding within living bodies of caterpillars, or that a cat should play with mice. Not believing this, I see no necessity in the belief that the eye was expressly designed."[1]

Darwin exemplifies the person whose worldview is shaped by the problem of suffering. His theological struggle to reconcile suffering in nature with the God of the Bible was foundational to his theory of evolution.[2] Darwin is not alone in this quandary. Like Darwin, many people reject the Christian faith because the world is full of suffering and evil. A very public example of this crisis of faith is the late Charles Templeton. Templeton was a former Billy Graham evangelist associate who left the faith in part because he could not understand how a loving God would allow suffering.

For centuries, philosophers have grappled with reconciling the existence of God and the prevalence of suffering in the world. As early as the third century BC, the Greek philosopher Epicurus wrote, "If God wants to prevent evil but cannot, he is not omnipotent, if he is powerful enough to prevent evil but will not, he is not benevolent; if he neither can nor desires to prevent evil, there is no good reason to think of him as 'divine' at all; if he both can and wishes to prevent evil, there is no way to account for its presence in our experience; thus, since evil clearly does exist, we must conclude that no omnipotent and omnibenevolent God exists."

David Hume, the eighteenth century philosopher, congealed the problem of evil to its essence when he asked, "Is [God] willing to prevent evil, but not able? Then he is impotent. Is he able, but not willing? Then he is malevolent. Is he both able and willing? Whence then is evil?"[3] The challenge of Hume is a valid issue that must be addressed within the Christian worldview.

---

[1] Charles Darwin in a letter dated May 22, 1860, taken from *Letters to Asa Gray.*

[2] This theme is developed in the book *Darwin's God: Evolution and the Problem of Evil* by Cornelius G. Hunter, Brazos Press, 2001.

[3] David Hume, *Dialogues Concerning Natural Religion,* ed. Norman Kemp Smith, New York: Thomas Nelson & Sons, 1947, p. 196.

More than merely questioning the origin of suffering, the more pressing question is the continued prevalence of suffering. Our biblical worldview must explain why God did not prevent the origin of suffering as well as why He permits it today. Hume's challenge will serve as a litmus test for evaluating various responses to the problem of suffering.

A Small God

The Perfect Paradise Paradigm provides a compelling answer to the problem of evil and suffering. Young earth creationism flatly rejects the idea that suffering was part of God's original "very good" creation. The Creator bears no responsibility for the origin of suffering in the Perfect Paradise theodicy.[4] Evil and suffering were brought about strictly by the rebellion of the creatures.

Mirroring Hume's approach, James Stambaugh of The Institute for Creation Research asserts that an ancient creation results in a theological impasse:

> If God created a world in which the creatures that inhabit it must suffer from evil (at least physical and emotional), then this evil has been present from the very beginning. This means that God is either powerless to do away with this kind of world or that He enjoys seeing His creatures suffer. A god who could create the world "subjected to vanity and corruption" is exactly like all the other gods of the ancient world—cruel, vicious, and capricious. In short, this god is not the God of the Bible.[5]

---

[4]A theodicy is a defense of God's goodness in light of suffering and evil.

[5] Stambaugh, James, "Creation and the Curse," Impact Article No. 272, The Institute for Creation Research, February 1996.

Identifying animal suffering with evil, this view assumes that God would not permit animals to suffer in a "very good" world. It is this sentiment—that God would not create a world where animals suffered and call it "very good"—that fuels the fire against the notion of an ancient creation. So strong is this sentiment that if God created life on earth long before He created Adam, young earth creationism says that God must be "cruel, vicious, and capricious."

Proponents of young earth creationism agree with Hume that God's character demands that He would not willingly permit suffering if the world continued as He originally intended. He permits suffering today only because His original intent was thwarted, and His "very good" world was ruined by man. Henry Morris makes it clear that the distinction between the worldviews is centered on the Creator's purpose for creation when he asks, "What conceivable purpose could God have had in interposing a billion years of suffering and death in the animal kingdom prior to implementing His great plan of salvation for lost men and women? He is neither cruel nor capricious, and would never be guilty of such pointless sadism."[6] Choosing to presume that God's original intent was a perfect world, Morris cannot conceive of a purpose for an ancient creation. Morris echoes Hume when he impugns the God of an old earth as cruel, capricious, and guilty of pointless sadism.

Such strong and heated language is understandable. Indeed, the same sentiment drove Darwin to his evolutionary worldview. Darwin agreed with young earth creationism that a supremely good Creator would not fashion a world with suffering and animal death if He were able to prevent it. Both would agree: "Surely He could devise a better plan than this."[7] It simply stains their im-

---

[6] Morris, Henry, "Christ and the Time of Creation," *Back To Genesis*, No. 70a, October 1994, The Institute of Creation Research.

[7] Morris, Henry, "Old-Earth Creationism," *Back To Genesis*, No. 100a, April, 1997, The Institute of Creation Research.

age of the Creator to assume that suffering and disasters in nature would have been part of His creation. God's will must have been for there to be no suffering because He called His perfect creation "very good." This unblemished embodiment of God's ideal intentions could have had no evil or suffering. It was a Perfect Paradise.

At this point we must make room for the transcendence of God and allow for mystery in His ways. Darwin, Templeton, and others who reject the faith simply cannot believe in a God who doesn't act in a way they think He should. Young earth creationism promotes this same sentiment: "One of the hardest things to understand is how anyone who claims to believe in a God of love can also believe in the geological ages, with their supposed record of billions of years of suffering and death before sin came into the world. This seems clearly to make God a God of waste and cruelty rather than a God of wisdom and power and love."[8]

Herein lies the fundamental difference between the two creation paradigms. If God created the world over billions of years and permitted hunger, asteroid bombardment, volcanoes and extinctions before man was created, it means He was willing to permit suffering in His original creation. Old earth creationists must explain why God would permit suffering in His original creation if he were able to prevent it.

Heated rhetoric notwithstanding, the Bible clearly teaches that not all suffering is pointless. There is indeed a conceivable purpose for why God would permit suffering apart from the sin of man. There is a better response to the problem of suffering, one that does not blame it solely on the creature nor compromise the power or character of the Creator.

---

[8] Morris, Henry, "The Fall, the Curse, and Evolution," *Back To Genesis*, No. 112a, April 1998.

For the Perfect Purpose Paradigm, the answer is not God's lack of ability to prevent the occurrence of evil. Rather, the answer lies with resolving His goodness with His willingness to permit suffering apart from the sin of man. The Bible emphatically states that God willingly permits suffering for a brief time in order to accomplish a perfect, eternal purpose. There is a greater good than preventing all suffering at all times.

Types of Worlds

Nature is aptly described by Tennyson as "red in tooth and claw." Suffering, hunger, and "survival of the fittest" describe the brutal existence in the animal kingdom. Extinctions testify that the record of nature is a long history of animal death. Mother nature demonstrates her temper with tornados, hurricanes, earthquakes, volcanoes, and floods. It is easy to think that a loving God would not consider this world to be very good. But that is exactly the words the Creator uses to describe His completed creation before the fall. Would God have created a world that included suffering and death and still consider that "very good?"

To better understand how a world such as ours would be consistent with the Master's plan, we must consider what options were at the Creator's disposal when He set out to create a "very good" world. The Creator had four options when it came to formulating a plan for creation.[9] He could:

1. Create no world at all,
2. Create a world without free moral creatures,
3. Create a world with free moral creatures that do not sin, or
4. Create a world with free moral creatures that do sin.

---

[9] Geisler, p. 51–52.

By His very nature God is free to choose as He pleases. Therefore, his motivation for creation was entirely innate to Himself. Out
of His perfection, self-sufficiency, and self-determination arose the
motivation for His free choice. With such freedom, God has chosen
that his providential and creative action demonstrate His own glory.
This notion lies at the heart of historic, evangelical theology.[10]

Logically speaking, God could have chosen to create no world
at all (option 1), but fortunately for us that was not His choice. We
may quickly and reasonably infer that choosing to not create a
world at all would not have achieved His purpose. He also could
have chosen to create a world without moral creatures (option 2).
God could have created a universe full of planets with vegetation
and amoral animals, but this would not have achieved His ultimate end in any significant way. Plant and animal life simply lack
the means with which to respond to God's glory.

It is logically possible that God could have created a world with
free moral creatures that only choose to do right (option 3). But
even though that might be logically possible, it may not be actually
realizable. For if the freedom of the creatures is true and complete,
then there is no way for God to ensure that the creatures will always
do right. If the circumstances of that world were ordered so that
the creatures always chose according to the Creator's intent, then
the creatures could not truly be free. If the Creator intervened to
prevent the creatures from acting wrongly, then that intervention
would be a violation of the creature's free will. Hence it is arguable
that the Creator could not create a world in which His free moral
creatures would not sin even though the existence of such a world
is a logical possibility.

So we are left with option four. God created a world in which
He could have a loving relationship with free, moral creatures

---

[10] See for example Jonathon Edwards' classic essay, *The End for Which We
Were Created.*

bearing His own image. This is what we find in Scripture, and this is the most logical of our four options. The best way to understand this is to examine the meaning of a loving relationship.

A meaningful love relationship is one where the object of love freely returns love. But the price of freely reciprocated love is the risk of rejection. Rare indeed is the individual who experiences love without first surviving the heartache of rejection. As C. S. Lewis wrote in *The Four Loves*, "the only place outside Heaven where you can be perfectly safe from all the dangers and perturbations of love is Hell." What is true for the creature is also true for the Creator. If Adam was free to choose to love God and obey Him, then he must also have been free to reject Him. For the choice between good and evil to be real, the real possibility for evil had to exist. If evil and suffering were not possible, then man would not truly be free to choose to love God. Only in this type of creation is God truly able to fulfill his purposes.

The Justification of God

A significant contribution to reconciling the problem of God and the existence of evil comes from the German philosopher and mathematician Gottfried Wilhelm Leibniz (1646–1716). [11] His logical approach to the problem of evil gives insight into why God would create a world like ours. Essentially, Leibniz states that although God is omnipotent, He was constrained to create a world that was logically possible, for even God cannot do what is logically impossible because to do otherwise would be nonsensical. Leibniz goes on to argue that this world is the best of all possible worlds. While his solution falls short of a satisfactory answer

---

[11] An explanation of how God can be good and powerful even though there is evil and suffering in the world is known as a theodicy, or a justification of God.

because of the various aspects of this world that in themselves are not good, Leibniz pioneers a way in which God can be justified.

If the notion of good is broadened to include the world to come, the argument becomes more appealing. Thomas Aquinas took this approach when he argued that this world is not necessarily the best of all possible worlds, but it is the best way to the best possible world. This world was created as the best means to the best end. Thus evil and suffering do not have to be resolved in this world alone. Geisler states the implication clearly: "Perhaps there is no better way for an all-loving, all-powerful God to defeat evil and produce a greater good than for Him to permit this present evil world."[12]

In the same way, the meaning of "very good" should be broadened beyond the garden to include God's entire plan for creation. Aquinas' theodicy answers the question as to what God meant when He declared His finished work of creation to be "very good." Not only does this world enable God to have a freely reciprocated love relationship with His image-bearers; but more importantly, it brings glory to the Creator. In light of the Creator's transcendence, it is perfectly plausible that this world is the perfect temporal means to accomplish the Master's perfect eternal purpose. There is a conceivable purpose for why God would permit animal suffering in His original, "very good" world. His ultimate purpose is not for man to blissfully dwell in a pristine paradise—His end is His glory. The original creation was "very good" because it is an element of the best way to that end.

God's Plan for Suffering

Understandably, responses to the problem of suffering tend to focus on the individual who suffers. Christians often argue that

---

[12] Geisler, p. 45.

good will come to the person in some tangible or intangible way if they remain faithful while suffering. They may never understand it, but it will ultimately be the best *for them*. Yet the Bible provides another perspective on suffering, one that emphasizes the outworking of God's eternal plan rather than the temporal good of the individual. As Paul wrote to the Romans, "all things work together for good to those who love God . . . according to His purpose" (Romans 8:28). It is not merely the good of the individual that is brought about; it is the good purpose of God that is brought to fruition. And that good purpose will not be completely realized until the plan has been completed.

More than anything else, the Perfect Paradise Paradigm is an attempt to answer the problem of suffering. Young earth creationists agree with Darwin and Hume that if God were good then His intent would be the prevention of suffering. It is exactly at this point that the mistake is made. What must be recognized is that God has a higher purpose for this creation than the prevention of suffering and evil. The problem of suffering and evil in this world must be understood from the perspective of God's eternal purpose for creation.

The Perfect Paradise Paradigm resolves the problem of suffering by blaming the victim. All suffering is due either directly to the actions of the sufferer or indirectly to the fall of Adam. But this is not the perspective of the Bible. Jesus' disciples made this same error when they assumed that a blind man suffered either because of his sin or that of his ancestors (with Adam being the ultimate ancestor). When they passed the blind man, they said to Jesus, "'Rabbi, who sinned, this man or his parents, that he would be born blind?' Jesus answered, 'It was neither that this man sinned, nor his parents; but it was so that the works of God might be displayed in him,'" (John 9:2–3).

God's plan for this man's life was that He might be glorified through his healing. His lifelong suffering was not caused by sin—it was ordained by God as a means to His ultimate end. Jesus drove this point home to His followers in an object lesson on suffering and repentance. He said that the accidental death of eighteen people on whom the tower of Siloam fell was not because of their sin (Luke 13:1–5). The same can be said for the ones in the two towers that fell two thousand years later in New York City. As Jesus made clear, the purpose of this creation is "that the works of God might be displayed."

Peter describes the proper biblical perspective that suffering can be due either to a person's guilt or to the plan of God.

> Beloved, do not be surprised at the fiery ordeal among you, which comes upon you for your testing, as though some strange thing were happening to you; but to the degree that you share the sufferings of Christ, keep on rejoicing so that also at the revelation of His glory, you may rejoice with exultation. If you are reviled for the name of Christ, you are blessed, because the Spirit of glory and of God rests upon you. [Make sure that] none of you suffer[s] as a murderer, or thief, or evildoer, or a troublesome meddler; but if anyone suffers as a Christian, [he is not to be] ashamed, but is to glorify God in this name. . . . Therefore, those also who suffer according to the will of God shall entrust their souls to a faithful Creator in doing what is right. (1 Peter 4:12–16, 19)

"Suffer according to the will of God"—herein is a clear indication that God permits suffering in this life as a means to accomplish His ultimate end, namely His glory.[13] Those who share the sufferings of Christ can take comfort in the fact that they will also share

---

[13] Note that the fall did not legitimize the use of suffering by God for His purposes. God's nature does not change and the fall did not enable Him to act in a way that would be contrary to His nature otherwise.

in His glory. This is the truth that enabled the faith of the saints chronicled in the eleventh chapter of Hebrews.

Focal Points

The two creation paradigms offer diametrically different perspectives on the problem of suffering. The Perfect Paradise Paradigm views suffering in light of the past. All suffering is traceable back to the original sin of Adam in the garden. It was never God's intent for His creation to suffer or be blemished in any way because He created it to be "very good." In stark contrast, the Perfect Purpose Paradigm sees suffering in light of the future. God has a plan, and history is unfolding in a providentially directed process that will ultimately accomplish His eternal purpose. Until the end, the plan will not be complete and the purpose will not be fully accomplished.

The sufferings of the present should not to be compared to the former paradise of Eden but rather to the future "glory that is to be revealed to us." Indeed all of creation groans in eager expectation of the coming fulfillment of God's perfect plan (Romans 8:18, 19). But for now, God chooses to permit suffering for a time in order to accomplish an eternal purpose. Suffering in this life can only be reconciled from the eternal perspective of the Master's plan.

Francis Anderson eloquently describes the contrast between these two perspectives on suffering in his introduction to Spurgeon's *The Suffering of Man and the Sovereignty of God*:

> Men seek an explanation of suffering in cause and effect. They look backwards for a connection between prior sin and present suffering. The Bible looks forwards (sic) in hope and seeks explanations, not so much in origins as in goals. The purpose of suffering is seen, not in its cause, but in its result. The man was born blind so that the works of God could be displayed in him (John 9:3). . . . We have to be as patient as God

Himself to see the end result, or to go on living in faith without seeing it.

The Scriptures teach that the answer to suffering is to have an eternal perspective. Our sufferings are light and momentary when compared to the eternal weight of glory that lies ahead. The philosophers are correct that God is not responsible for the origin of evil, but He is responsible for not preventing evil. He permits evil even in a "very good" world for a short time because He has a perfect, eternal purpose.

The Bible never suggests that it is God's plan to always prevent evil from affecting the lives of innocent people. This concept is very clearly demonstrated by Job. Job had done nothing to deserve the tragedy visited upon his life, yet God brought suffering upon him (Job 2:3). Job never understood why he had to experience such great suffering. In the end, God revealed His sovereignty to Job in a way that simply said, "Trust me." The same is true in our lives. We can be confident that God loves us deeply, that His plan is working, and that His ways are right even if in our perspective they don't appear to be.

DUST TO DUST 11

In previous chapters we established the biblical context for an ancient creation and critically examined the theological foundation for the young earth creationism worldview. It became clear that the conflict between the two paradigms is most apparent in the issue of suffering. The Perfect Paradise Paradigm provides an answer to the problem of suffering by envisioning an idyllic paradise with no suffering until the sin of man brought perfection to ruin. The Perfect Purpose Paradigm answers the problem of suffering by saying that this world is the best way to the best of all possible worlds.

Without question, the topic of original animal mortality is the flashpoint in the heated debate between these two paradigms. As such, it is important to address this issue in some depth. The death of animals will serve as an excellent case study to determine which paradigm best fits the truth revealed to us.

The Flashpoint

As if it were a direct indication of one's respect for the authority of the Scriptures and the character of God, animal immortality has become the litmus test of orthodoxy for young earth creationism apologists. As one example among many, consider the following statement: "Those who accept the Bible believe that death is a punishment for sin; death must have come into existence after Adam fell."[1]

Considering the possibility of animal death before the creation of Adam is equated to rejecting the authority and veracity of Scripture. It is as though belief in animal immortality is necessary for one to believe in the truth of the Bible. It is important, then, to demonstrate the fallacy of this assertion.

Within the camp of Perfect Paradise proponents, the theological weapon of choice against the theory of evolution is the claim that the Bible teaches the earth was created too recently to permit evolution. But because linguistic studies and proper exegesis suggest that the author of Genesis may have been speaking of longer periods than 24 hours for the six days of creation, biblical proof that the earth is young is said to come from the original immortality of animals. For this reason, a leading proponent of the young earth paradigm writes, "Animal death, as well as human death, entered the world only when man brought sin into the world (Romans 5:12). This is one very cogent reason why Bible-believing Christians should reject the concept of long geological ages."[2] Animal immortality therefore becomes the theological wedge that marginalizes all other biblical and scientific evidence about the antiquity of the earth. The issue of animal immortality provides theological proof that the earth is young and hence that evolution is false.

Unfortunately, the strong language in this family squabble has brought division in churches today. Some church leaders consider

---

[1] Stambaugh, James, "Death Before Sin?" Impact Article No. 191, The Institute for Creation Research, May 1989.

[2] Morris, Henry, "Adam and the Animals," Impact Article No. 212, The Institute for Creation Research, February 1991.

the possibility of long ages of creation to be a compromise to biblical truth and essential doctrine. Some go so far in their rhetoric as to threaten that a creation paradigm allowing the death of animals before the sin of Adam will "stain God's true glory, majesty and power."[3] On the fringe of demagoguery, the audacious claim has been made that animal death prior to Adam's sin makes God out to be "cruel . . . capricious . . . [and] guilty of pointless sadism."[4]

Healthy Reminders

Because of heated rhetoric such as this, people often dismiss the possibility of animal death without considering the details of the issue. Some fear that considering ideas such as animal death before the fall would put one on a slippery slope to evolution and atheism. Yet the Bible urges us to test all things. Charges of this magnitude should be either clearly established in Scripture or else strongly refuted. The issue of animal immortality will be critically examined in the following chapters in the hope of bringing peace, unity, and civility to this factious topic for the family of God.

As we continue let us remember that God has not told us everything there is to know. He has given us sufficient revelation to merit belief, but He has also preserved the mystery that legitimizes faith's reward. He reserves the right to operate in ways that are different from what we would do or anticipate Him to do. Let us gird our minds for action and test these issues to see if they are true. Our transcendent God is greatly to be praised, worthy to be loved with all of our minds, and deserving of our trust.

---

[3] Van Bebber and Taylor, p. 22.

[4] Morris, Henry, "Christ and the Time of Creation," *Back To Genesis*, No. 70a, The Institute of Creation Research, October 1994.

Summary of the Biblical Arguments

Essentially every book or article written about a recent creation of the earth is based on the theological framework of the Perfect Paradise Paradigm. That paradigm asserts that creation was rapid and recent and thus there was no animal death before the fall. Indeed, a key biblical proof for a young earth comes from the issue of animal immortality. Those biblical arguments fall along four lines:[5]

Claim 1: The penalty of the curse included animal death in a fallen creation.

Claim 2: The doctrine of atonement depends on original animal immortality.

Claim 3: Animal death and suffering could not be considered "very good" by a loving, wise, and merciful Creator.

Claim 4: All animals were created as herbivores and commanded to be vegetarians.

The first claim will be addressed in this chapter with separate chapters devoted to consider each of the remaining claims.

The First Claim:
The Penalty of the Curse Included Animal Death in a Fallen Creation

The Christian will recognize the current state of things to have been affected by the curse on all creation in Genesis 3:14–19, with the 'wages of sin' pronounced

---

[5] For example, see Van Bebber and Taylor, "Creation and Time: A Report on the Progressive Creationist Book by Hugh Ross," Eden Productions, 1994 and Morris, Henry III, *After Eden: Understanding Creation, the Curse, and the Cross*, Master Books, 2003.

on all of Adam's dominion because of his rebellion. In the beginning, there was no carnivorous activity (Genesis 1:30), no extinction, no decay, no cancer. But now, everywhere we look we see sin's effect.[6]

How does the Christian religion understand death? . . . Evidently, man and all animals possessing true life in the Biblical sense . . . were created to live forever . . . the lie was believed, the penalty for sin denied, and sin entered the world. The resultant curse on all of creation was the curse of death, and touched not only mankind— "for dust thou art, and unto dust shalt thou return" (Genesis 3:19)—but the animals (v. 14), the plants (v. 18), and even the earth itself (v. 17).[7]

The Response

After Adam succumbed to temptation and ate the forbidden fruit, God confronted him and pronounced the curse. The curse has become a blank check within young earth creationism to explain away everything unseemly in life. The language of the curse has been generalized to be all-inclusive. But when put to the test, the curse pronounced in the six verses of Genesis 3:14–19 is very specific and focused in scope. The curse was explicitly directed to the serpent, to the woman, and finally to the man. While the consequences of the curse broadly impact the creation through the fallen nature of man, it neither brought about animal death nor a wholesale physical change to the constitution of nature in general.

---

[6] Morris, John, "What Could the God of Scripture Call 'Very Good?'" *Back To Genesis*, No. 145b, The Institute for Creation Research, January 2001.

[7] Morris, John, "Evolution and the Wages of Sin," Impact Article No. 209, The Institute for Creation Research, November 1990.

Scope of the Curse

The curse was initially addressed to the serpent, then to the woman, and finally to the man. In each case, the punishment fits the crime.

God begins the curse by addressing the serpent.

> The LORD God said to the serpent,
> "Because you have done this,
> Cursed are you more than all cattle,
> And more than every beast of the field;
> On your belly you will go,
> And dust you will eat
> All the days of your life;
> And I will put enmity
> Between you and the woman,
> And between your seed and her seed;
> He shall bruise you on the head,
> And you shall bruise him on the heel."

There are three aspects to the serpent's punishment, each directly related to the privileged position of the serpent. First, having been distinguished as "more crafty than any beast of the field" (3:1), the serpent was humiliated and consigned to crawl on its belly all its life. Beginning from an exalted position, the nemesis was humiliated lower than the creation over which it had previously been exalted. Second, the serpent's humiliation is apparent in that it is forced to eat dust. Eating dust is a common figure for humiliation and is a reflection of the nature of the temptation the serpent posed to Eve. Since the fall forced man to return to the dust, eating dust was a constant reminder of his guilt. The fate of the serpent to be crushed by the foot of man is the last word on the serpent's short-lived triumph in the garden.[8]

---

[8] Mathews, p. 244.

It is important to recognize that this was no ordinary serpent.[9] More than just a snake, the serpent in the garden embodied the person of Satan.[10] God's condemnation of the serpent in Genesis 3:14 is not directed at the species in general or at the animal specifically but at the nemesis it represents. The fire of Satan's rebellion against God was stoked by pride in that he believed he could tempt Eve just as he had been tempted. Thus his punishment was to be humiliation and ultimate subjection under the foot of Jesus (1 Corinthians 15:25). The extent of the punishment was to crawl on his belly and eat dust "all the days of [his] life," a foreshadowing of the humiliation and eventual demise of Satan. Having swelled up in pride and challenged God's authority, he would be humiliated and all his authority would be stripped from him. His run at the throne would be short-lived and his destruction complete. His days would be numbered, and his life would soon end. In the curse on the serpent we see an indication that all was proceeding according to the eternal plan of God.

If the animals were immortal before the curse and sentenced to death at the curse, the proof is not found in this passage. The curse did not apply to the entire animal kingdom or to any specific animal but rather to the evil one embodied in the serpent. Cattle and the beasts of the field are mentioned only as a point of reference to indicate the exalted height from which the evil one fell.[11] Including the cattle and

---

[9] Leland, *Answer to Christianity as Old as the Creation*, Dublin, 1733, vol. ii., p. 516. "If there was a real serpent made use of, yet still it may be supposed that the curse was only and properly directed and designed against Satan, who actuated that creature, though couched in terms accommodated to the condition of the creature he actuated and assumed."

[10] Mathews, p. 234.

[11] As an example, consider the greeting given by Elizabeth to Mary when she was pregnant with Jesus. When Elizabeth said, "You are blessed by God above all other women," (NLT) she did not mean that all women were specifically blessed by God at the time of Mary's conception, but just not as much as Mary. Likewise, for the serpent to be cursed more than all the beasts does not mean that they were cursed along with the serpent.

beasts for comparison does not mean that those species (much less all species) were literally included in the curse with the serpent.

Although the Perfect Paradise Paradigm assumes that all carnivores were herbivores before the fall, there simply is no indication in the curse of the serpent that the entire animal kingdom underwent a total systemic anatomical, behavioral, and biological change at the fall.[12]

Next God addresses the curse to the woman.

> To the woman He said,
> "I will greatly multiply
> Your pain in childbirth,
> In pain you will bring forth children;
> Yet your desire will be for your husband,
> And he will rule over you."

As with the serpent, here again the punishment is related to the primary privileges and responsibilities of the woman. Recall that Adam exalted his wife with the name Eve, which means "life" or "life-producer," because she was given the unique privilege of being the mother of all humanity (Genesis 3:20). Because her exalted position was based in part on her role in childbirth, her punishment was related to childbirth as well. The increased pain in childbirth would serve as a reminder throughout all generations of her role in the fall.

She had also been created as Adam's partner. Adam was to relate to Eve with a gracious, sacrificial love that considered her interests more important than his own. Adam lovingly exercised

---

[12] Some have suggested that the serpent originally crawled on four legs and then lost them in the curse, but that is simply reading into the text to justify a presumption. The curse of crawling is symbolic in nature—it does not indicate a new characteristic as much as a new significance to the crawling. Kidner (p. 70) suggests that the crawling is much like the rainbow in Genesis 9:13 where a new significance, not a new existence is granted to the rainbow.

his authority over her by giving her an exalting name. Before the fall, that authority was an ennobling virtue, exercised to bless and exalt his partner. But the fall interrupted that embodiment of divine love. Sin profoundly affected her relationship with her husband and the marital relationships of all her progeny. The exact implications of the curse have been debated through the ages, but it is clear that sin brought estrangement and difficulty to the blessed estate of marriage that, in its ultimate realization, serves as a metaphor of the unity between Christ and His church. Sin brought enmity where once there was holy unity.

After directly addressing the serpent and the woman, the curse is finally addressed to Adam.

> Then to Adam He said,
> 'Because you have listened to the voice of your wife, and have eaten from the tree about which I commanded you, saying,
> "You shall not eat from it";
> Cursed is the ground because of you."

It is quite significant that God does not directly address the ground, for the ground had committed no offense. God is speaking to Adam when He says, "Cursed is the ground because of you." The ground is not directly cursed. Through the effects of sin on Adam, the ground is indirectly affected. The ground is indirectly cursed because humans are now sinful.

Like the presumption that the curse applied to the animal kingdom in general, some argue that all of nature and its laws were cursed as well. Yet Adam was simply told, "Cursed is the ground because of you." There is no indication that the physical processes set in motion when God created the earth were altered by the sin of Adam. Indeed, the Scriptures teach that the laws of nature themselves have not changed since they were first created.[13] The curse simply indicates that the ground would suffer the consequences of Adam's sin.

To understand the curse on the ground, it must be understood in the context of Genesis 1:28–29 where God commands man to have dominion over creation and subdue the land. Adam is incapable of carrying out the mandate of God in his fallen state. Hence the ground is cursed because it is not subdued or adequately maintained by man in his fallen state.[14]

The sobering pronouncement against Adam continues.

. . . In toil you will eat of it
All the days of your life.
Both thorns and thistles it shall grow for you;
And you will eat the plants of the field;
By the sweat of your face
You will eat bread,
Till you return to the ground,
Because from it you were taken;
For you are dust,
And to dust you shall return.

Adam's privileges would now become his problems. Before the fall, working the land to eat of its produce was a joyful task.

---

[13] God's unchanging nature and His covenant faithfulness are demonstrated by analogy to the immutable laws of physics. (Hodge, p. 539; Ross, Hugh, *Matter of Days*, NavPress, 2004, p. 87 and 106.) For example, see Jeremiah 33:19–26 where God says the covenant with Israel will not change unless the fixed laws of the heavens change. See also Jeremiah 31:36 and Psalms 89:30–37.

[14] According to Kidner, "Thorns and thistles are eloquent signs of nature untamed and encroaching; in the Old Testament they mark the scenes of man's self-defeat and God's judgment, e.g. in the sluggard's field (Proverbs 24:31) and the ruined city (Isaiah 34:13). They need not be envisaged here as newly created, but as henceforth a perennial threat (as the unconquered Canaanites would be to Israel, Numbers 33:55); for man in his own disorder would never now 'subdue' the earth." Kidner, p. 72.

But after the fall, the fulfilling work would become painful toil. Because of sin, Adam would be exiled from the garden and his stewardship over the ground would be laborious. Adam would now be forced to encounter a very different world than the garden paradise fashioned for him and his bride. Thorns and thistles would be a constant nemesis to him. The ground that had been a medium of joyful service to God would become an adversary in Adam's struggle to survive.

Not only will his days become difficult, they will also be numbered. God told Adam that his toil would continue "till [he returned] to the ground." The final toll of the curse is a resounding sentence of death. Adam would return to the ground, for from the ground he had been taken. With this pronouncement, God executed the sentence for which Adam had been warned.

Focal Points

The curse serves to illustrate the distinction between man and animal in the garden. The promise of life and the curse of death had been set before man in the center of the garden. Fruit from the Tree of Life was his for the taking as long as he abstained from the forbidden tree. These trees bore great significance for Adam, but not for the animals. There was no promise of life or curse of death for the animals in the center of the garden. Blessing and curse were there only for the ones created in the image of the Maker.

Indeed death did enter with the curse, but it was directed specifically at man. The trees were not put into the garden for the animals. Because they are not moral creatures, the animals were free to eat from either of the trees without consequence. There is no reason to assume that they were not free to remain in the garden after the expulsion of Adam and Eve. The angel was sent only to prevent Adam and Eve from returning to the garden and having access to the Tree of Life. The angel was not sent to bar animals from the tree. Neither eternal life nor the curse was intended for the animals.

The end of the curse arrives without mention of animal death. God cursed the serpent, the woman, and the man. In each case the punishment fit the crime. Although many have inferred that God intended animals to die along with Adam, this is not what God said. Speaking directly to Adam, God said "you" will die; He did not say the animals would die as well. To include animal death in the curse is to add to the Scriptures. Advocates of the Perfect Paradise Paradigm must look elsewhere to justify the notion of original animal immortality.

RANKING THE REVELATIONS

The cornerstone of young earth creationism theology is the notion that God cursed the entire creation after the fall of man. After God finished, it was "very good"; after Adam had finished, it became the world we live in today. Ultimately, blame is laid at the feet of Adam for all pain and suffering.

When young earth apologists look for the smoking gun to prove that the curse changed the world from a Perfect Paradise to the world of today, they look to the New Testament and Paul's letter to the Romans: "For the anxious longing of the creation waits eagerly for the revealing of the sons of God. For the creation was subjected to futility, not willingly, but because of Him who subjected it, in hope that the creation itself also will be set free from its slavery to corruption into the freedom of the glory of the children of God. For we know that the whole creation groans and suffers the pains of childbirth together until now" (Romans 8:19–22).

This passage stands with Genesis 1:31 as a pillar of young earth creationism. The entire creation falls within one of two extremes with the curse as the line of demarcation. Before the fall, all was sheer perfection because it was very good. After the fall, everything is futile and decaying. These two pillars supposedly describe the mutually exclusive and polar opposite conditions that completely encompass the young earth creationism paradigm.

Two essential elements of the Perfect Paradise Paradigm are supported by these two pillars. First, if the world before the fall was absolutely perfect, then God is not responsible for suffering. Everything that is unseemly about the world today is included in the futility and decay which was brought about by man's rebellion. Second, since the entire universe is now corrupt and futile, all scientific observations—and scientists themselves—are suspect.

With these pillars, young earth creationism provides answers to the problem of suffering and the problematic evidence of an ancient creation. Upon closer inspection, however, these pillars turn out to be full of cracks.

Incorruptible Truth: Revelation and the Fall

The letter to the Hebrews opens with a declaration that God has truthfully revealed Himself throughout history in many different ways. One generation in particular had the privilege to say, "The Word became flesh and dwelt among us, and we beheld His glory" (John 1:14). His Word to us today was breathed through the authors of the Scriptures. This "special revelation" is an inerrant, infallible library of sixty-six books, written over hundreds of years by authors from diverse occupations, backgrounds, and languages. Remarkably, they all speak a single, true, and consistent message, inspired by the Author of all revelation.

In addition to the Son and the Scriptures, the Creator has also spoken through His creation. Theologians describe the witness of nature as "general revelation." Those who did not see Jesus, or hear His story told, or read His written Word have a clear and true—although limited—testimony through what He has made. A voice from heaven bids every person to "lift up [their] eyes on high and see who has created these stars" (Isaiah 40:26).

A Witness to All Generations

There have always been people outside the reach of the written Word. Many civilizations have risen and subsequently passed into history without hearing the name of Jesus or reading the written Word of God. So what about those who have never heard? This is no excuse, for Scripture says that they have heard the Word of God through creation. As the Psalmist has written:

> The heavens are telling of the glory of God;
> And their expanse is declaring the work of His hands.
> Day to day pours forth speech,
> And night to night reveals knowledge.
> There is no speech, nor are there words;
> Their voice is not heard.
> Their line has gone out through all the earth,
> And their utterances to the end of the world.
> (Psalm 19:1–4a)

The heavens are a wordless testimony to the glory of God. Day after day, night after night, creation utters its mighty declaration of the Creator's glory. Creation provides evidence of a supremely wise, powerful, and benevolent Creator who providentially crafted life and our unique place in the cosmos. The revelation in nature is as perfect as the Law of the Lord (spoken of later in Psalm 19), only the content and the medium of the messages differ.

No nation or generation in the history of humanity has been left without a witness. Throughout history God has clearly revealed Himself, and yet He has allowed men the freedom to follow Him or reject His message (Acts 14:16–17). Perhaps the most striking text that addresses the rejection of God's witness in nature is found in Paul's letter to the Romans. In verses 19–20 of the first chapter, Paul emphasizes the significance of God's truth revealed in nature: "For the wrath of God is revealed from heaven against all ungodliness and unrighteousness of men who suppress the truth in unrighteousness, because that which is known about

God is evident within them; for God made it evident to them. For since the creation of the world His invisible attributes, His eternal power and divine nature, have been clearly seen, being understood through what has been made, so that they are without excuse."

Four significant points are made in this passage. First, the attributes of God are "invisible": we cannot observe God through a telescope; we cannot weigh Him on a set of scales; we cannot place Him on a slide under a microscope. We only know about God by the things He chooses to reveal to us through His word and "through what has been made." Second, nature has revealed the Creator from the very beginning. Even before man was on the scene, nature has revealed God's truth. Third, the revelation of nature is "clearly seen," "evident," and "understood by all." Men do not lack a witness, nor do they fail to understand the witness. There is no need for a preacher or a prophet to make the message from observable creation understood. Fourth, God reveals His wrath from heaven against those who reject His natural revelation.

Taken together, these four points illuminate the Perfect Paradise Paradigm's misconception about the reliability of revelation in nature after the fall. There is no problem with the transmission or the reception of the clear message from God through nature. Rather, the problem lies in the response to the message—the suppression of the truth in unbelief. The error of wicked men is not due to God's failure to communicate, it is strictly due to the willful suppression of the truth that they clearly see but do not see fit to acknowledge.

Two Books

Revelation in nature is a topic that is rich in significance with respect to the historical roots of orthodox theology. In the oldest doctrinal confession within Reformed Theology we find a strong endorsement of the "two books of revelation." Entitled "The Means by Which We Know God," Article 2 of the Belgic Confession (1561) states:

We know him by two means: First, by the creation, preservation, and government of the universe, since that universe is before our eyes like a beautiful book in which all creatures, great and small, are as letters to make us ponder the invisible things of God: his eternal power and his divinity, as the apostle Paul says in Romans 1:20. All these things are enough to convict men and to leave them without excuse. Second, he makes himself known to us more openly by his holy and divine Word, as much as we need in this life, for his glory and for the salvation of his own.

Not all theologians have agreed on this "two books" view. On one extreme, Karl Barth dismissed nature entirely as an independent source of revelation. Barth argued that a second source of knowledge detracted from the "absolute uniqueness and unrepeatableness of God's revelation in Jesus Christ."[1] The majority of Reformed theologians, however, have concurred with the Belgic Confession that God has truthfully revealed Himself through what He has made.

Young earth creationism proponents line up with Barth in rejecting nature as a reliable source of revelation. They do so not out of Barth's fear of diminishing the significance of Christ's revelation, but because it contradicts their theology of creation.[2] This issue is a key flash point in the age of the earth debate as it associates an old earth perspective with the rejection of biblical authority.

---

[1] Berkouwer, Gerrit C., *General Revelation*, Eerdmans Pub Co., 1952, p. 24.

[2] Young earth creationists are philosophically aligned with Karl Barth when they reject nature as a source of true revelation in reaction to contemporary events. With the hindsight of history, it is evident that Barth's strong rejection of general revelation was at least in part a reaction to how the German church erroneously identified history with the voice of God at the time Hitler seized

Inerrancy and Interpretation

A fundamental axiom of young earth creationism is that the entire physical realm was cursed because of the sin of Adam. As a consequence, the facts of nature can supposedly only be understood when seen through the lens of Scripture. Although the piety of that perspective is appealing, to discount the truth that God has revealed in His creation is to stand in conflict with the truth of the Scriptures. A commitment to biblical inerrancy demands that God's message—one that is "understood through what has been made"—be infallibly correct.

God's nature demands that His revelation be untainted and free from error. Prophets of old were well aware of this necessity of inerrancy. The test of authenticity for a prophet was simple: God would not lie, so if a prophecy failed, it meant death to the false prophet.[3] For the same reason, the testimony of nature must be true and completely free of error. Since the Author of revelation cannot lie or contradict Himself, all revelation must be consistent. Both nature and the Bible must consistently speak one message. God Himself declares that, "the witness in the sky is faithful" (Psalm 89:37). There can therefore be no contradiction between the facts of nature and the facts of the Bible.[4]

---

power (see *Revelation and the Bible*, edited by Carl F. H. Henry, Baker Book House, 1958, p. 19). Barth rejected the idea that God revealed Himself through history because of "his passionate belief that historical scholarship cannot lay the basis for faith" (Alister McGrath, *Christian Theology*, Blackwell Publishers, 1997, p. 381). Likewise, young earth creationists reject scientific evidence for the earth's antiquity because they erroneously identify geologic ages with Darwin and his theory of evolution. In their paradigm, scientific inquiry cannot be a valid aid to biblical interpretation.

[3] Deuteronomy 18:20–22.

[4] Two good references for this line of reasoning are Geisler, Norman L., *Baker Handbook of Christian Apologetics*, and Ross, Hugh, *Matter of Days*, NavPress, 2004.

To rank the revelations of God is to compromise the very character of God. Nature must be an inerrant revelation because otherwise God would be unjust to hold people accountable on the basis of a flawed or deceptive revelation. If the so-called "fallen creation" were not a true witness, people would have an excuse for unbelief and a legitimate basis for appeal. Because all people that have ever lived—including those who have no knowledge of Scripture or prophetic revelation—are "without excuse," the revelation in nature must be fully inerrant and uncorrupted. Consistency of truth across all domains of revelation is demanded by a commitment to biblical inerrancy.

A Question of Authority

An important question and one on which conservative theologians differ is the proper relationship between scientific evidences and theological models. Often it is said by young earth creationists that this question is actually a question of authority. Most young earth creationism apologists insist that a clear reading of Scripture must always have authority over inferences from nature. This distinction is justified by asserting the propositional nature of special revelation—it consists of words that can be interpreted according to rules of grammar—and the presuppositional nature of general revelation which is understood in light of scientific presuppositions. Hence the potential for flawed presuppositions in the realm of science subordinates general revelation to the propositional statements of Scripture.

One must be careful in pressing this distinction too far. The Bible does not draw lines of demarcation between the various modes of God's self-revelation. Never do the sacred writers warn the reader that insights from nature must be filtered through the lens of Scripture. The Scriptures simply assert that God is the author of all revelation and God cannot lie. Luther and Calvin both affirmed that while partial and incomplete, the Creator's self-revelation in His creation was fully trustworthy and reliable. Knowledge of the Creator revealed in nature is reiterated and enhanced in Scripture.[5] Hence the correct distinction is not between Scripture and nature, it is between theologians and scientists.

Note also that this distinction between the propositional truth of Scripture and the presuppositional nature of general revelation is not universally valid. Presuppositions weigh heavily on biblical interpretation as well. Many false doctrines have arisen because proof texts were interpreted in light of a flawed paradigm. Indeed, systematic theology is a difficult and inexact science.[6] Scripture exhorts the Bible student to study and rightly divide the truth in order to gain the Author's approval (2 Timothy 2:15).

Conflict between science and theology does not necessarily mean that theology must trump science. Those who make this artificial distinction risk the error of hastily dismissing a mass of extra-biblical data (such as from science, history, or archeology) that could otherwise provide insight into passages with latitude of meaning or that are difficult to interpret (such as the length of days in Genesis 1).

Potential conflict is actually an opportunity for greater learning, for "when the revealed and the observed seem hard to combine, it is because we know too little, not too much."[7] J.I. Packer rightly notes that when properly understood, the facts of science should reinforce sound doctrine or aid us in correctly interpreting

---

[5] This principle does not imply that all truths in nature are more fully expressed in the Scriptures—there are many truths of creation that are revealed in more detail in nature than in Scripture. Matters such as the knowledge of God as Redeemer that are more completely revealed in Scripture.

[6] Hodge well states that "the Bible contains the truths which the theologian has to collect, authenticate, arrange, and exhibit in their internal relation to each other. . . . This is not an easy task, or one of slight importance" (Hodge, pp. 1, 2). Hodge goes on to say that we cannot merely assimilate the "mass of undigested facts," but rather it is necessary to systematize and reconcile the facts.

[7] Kidner, p. 30.

some difficult passages of Scripture. Packer writes, "It is tempting
. . . to deny the problem, either by discounting one or other set of
facts, or by locking them into separate compartments in our minds.
. . . The truth is that the facts of nature yield positive help in many
ways for interpreting Scripture statements correctly, and the dis-
cipline of wrestling with the problem of relating the two sets of
facts, natural and biblical, leads to a greatly enriched understanding of both."[8] This in no way diminishes the authority of Scripture;
it simply integrates the whole of God's revelation. Truth is not in
jeopardy when theologians and scientists differ. Wisdom would
have us discern which interpretation is most solidly established in
the revelation of God in Scripture and in nature.

A Futile and Corrupt Creation

Young earth creationism dismisses general revelation as a true
witness to the Creator by asserting that the entire creation is now
"fallen" and unfit as a reliable source of truth. Moreover, the futility
and corruption of creation spoken of by Paul in Romans 8:19–22
is associated with suffering, pain, animal death, and natural evil
(hurricanes, earthquakes, etc). All of these unseemly attributes of
the present world must be consequences of the curse because they
are anything but perfect.

But did Paul have cavities and carnivores in mind when he
spoke of futility and corruption? Was Paul describing the univer-
sal impact of the curse on creation? To answer these questions we
must look closely at the text and the context of this passage.

The Creation

Paul makes creation his focus in each of the four verses in
Romans 8. Creation is "anxiously longing" and "waits eagerly"

---

[8] Packer, J. I. *"Fundamentalism" and the Word of God*, I.V.F., 1958, p. 135.

(19); it was "subjected to futility" (20) and will be set free from "slavery to corruption" (21); and it "groans and suffers the pains of childbirth" (22). The Greek word used by Paul, *ktisis*, is found 20 times in the New Testament and is used to mean the created world (Romans 1:20), humanity (Colossians 1:23), and human institutions (1 Peter 2:13).

Futility

The Greek word in verse 20 translated variously as "futility, frustration, [or] vanity," is *mataiotes*, which can mean "emptiness [or] transience."[9] Interestingly, this word is used only three times in the New Testament, and the other two occasions describe the thoughts and actions of unbelievers. In neither of those two cases does it refer to a characteristic of inanimate creation.

Corruption

Paul expresses a parallel thought to describe the condition of creation in verse 21 when he uses the phrase "slavery to corruption." Similar to futility, the Greek word translated as corruption or decay is *phthora*, meaning destruction or a perishable quality, something that is wasting away. This word is used nine times in the New Testament, and like the other two cases of "futility," it always refers to people. Peter uses an almost identical phrase in 2 Peter 2:18–19 when he describes wicked people as "speaking out arrogant words of vanity (mataiotes) . . . while they themselves are slaves of corruption (phthora)."

From the usage of the words for futility and corruption, one can perhaps conclude that Paul is describing humanity rather than the entire creation. If that is the case, Paul is not ascribing all

---

[9] In the Greek Old Testament that Paul is familiar with and sometimes quotes from, *mataiotes* is a rendering of the Hebrew word *hebel* which often expresses the concept of transience. See Elbert, Paul, "Paul's Concept of the Death, Suffering, and Future of Humankind." To be published.

manner of decay and suffering in the material world to an action imposed at the curse. However, the consensus of theologians is that Paul is indeed referring to the entire created material world in this passage.

Paradise Lost

Because the words translated as futility and corruption have multiple meanings in other New Testament uses, the context of Paul's usage in Romans must be brought into consideration. At one end of the spectrum, young earth creationist scholars interpret Romans 8:19–22 in the broadest possible sense to encompass all unseemly aspects of the entire physical (and spiritual) realm. Futility, corruption, suffering, and groaning go beyond a personification of creation to the literal imputation of all decay, natural disasters, suffering, and physical death at the fall.

If such a broad impact of the curse were the case, one would expect that the curse itself would substantiate that presumption.[10] Instead, as we have seen, that simply is not the case. The ground is only indirectly addressed through the pronouncement against Adam. The animal kingdom in general is not mentioned in the curse. The laws of physics and the sun, moon, and stars are not included in the curse at all. Thus the broadest possible interpretation of Romans 8:19–22 is invoked by young earth creationism because it is required by the Perfect Paradise Paradigm.

As we have seen, Paul declares in Romans 1:20 that rejection of the revelation in nature is inexcusable because its message of truth has been clear and evident to all from the very beginning. In the tenth chapter Paul reasons that all have indeed heard God's

---

[10] If young earth creationists are correct that the punishment for sin included a wholesale change in the laws of physics and introduced every type of physical suffering, then perhaps God should have warned Adam to that effect. Certainly the scope of those effects extends much more broadly than "in the day that you eat from it you shall surely die" (Genesis 2:17).

message because the heavens are telling of His glory. In between these two passages, Paul says that the creation is "subjected to futility" and is in "slavery to corruption." Taken in context, he could not have meant that the natural realm was substantively and universally changed. Biblical inerrancy demands that Paul could not simultaneously claim that nature is a true revelation from God and that the message is corrupted. The unchanging laws of nature, the patterns of weather, and the constitution of the animal and plant kingdoms are all part of the whole creation that has made the Creator's attributes known since before the fall of man.

Paul's description of the present creation does not necessarily imply that all suffering and animal death came as a result of man's rebellion. Paul may have used futility and corruption in creation in a more limited way. Rather than describing the direct effects of the curse on the universe, Paul may have been describing the impact of man's sin on the world around him.

Old earth creationists readily agree that the sin sown by Adam reaped a horrific harvest on the world around him. After the fall, man no longer experienced an innocent nature, one in harmony with the Creator and His creation. Sin brought about frustration as Adam left the garden to subdue a hostile world. Adam was exiled from the pristine sanctity of his garden home to face the toilsome burden of cultivating and keeping the thorn-filled, rocky ground outside the boundaries of Eden. Originally given the mandate to subdue, cultivate, keep, and rule over the created world, man in his sinful state became derelict in his duties, and the entire creation has suffered the consequences.

There is also the possibility that the futility and corruption Paul describes are not a result of the curse at all. In addition to latitude about what is meant by futility and corruption, there is also latitude about when creation might have been subjected to futility and corruption. The Scriptures do not state explicitly when or why the subjection occurred. Futility and corruption could have been part of the creation from the very beginning. To understand why the Creator would subject His creation to futility and corruption and then call it "very good," we must consider the Creator's perfect and eternal purpose for creation.

A Perfect Purpose for Futility and Corruption

Before the history of humanity began, God planned the creation, redemption, and consummation of His kingdom. Our world was originally designed with built-in obsolescence because it was only needed for a time. Both redemption and consummation were providentially planned stages of history, and the world was created to accomplish that plan. The whole creation was both futile and hopeful because it was a temporal means to an eternal end.

The Motive for Subjection

In the context of the Creator's eternal purpose, a temporal, perishing creation is completely consistent with the Creator's character. This perspective is made clear in the NIrV rendering: "The created world was bound to fail. But that was not the result of its own choice. It was planned that way by the One who made it." (Romans 8:20 NIrV). Futility in the original creation actually demonstrates the sovereign nature of the Master who brought it about. Commenting on this passage, the theologian Donald Barnhouse says,

> The most important thought that comes out of all this is that the Lord God has control, even of the processes of death and decay. He created these processes for a distinct purpose, because he is bringing to pass a plan which includes the death of all things that are visible. When we see the horrible disintegration which surrounds us we may look up to Heaven with the calm certainty that God has never made any mistakes, but that He is proceeding by an ordered process of death and decay to bring about a definite purpose which He

has planned from all eternity. . . . Our text states flatly
that God cares, that God does have the power, but that
God is letting all things move into corruption because
He is working out an eternal purpose.[11]

From the sentimental perspective of young earth creationism,
God would not intentionally create a world with futility and corruption: "Surely He could devise a better plan than this."[12] But
Scripture is clear—creation was subjected to futility strictly because of God's choice. By virtue of His nature, His choice could
not have been better. While the Perfect Paradise Paradigm says
there must be a better way because a world with suffering and
animal mortality doesn't seem "very good," the Perfect Purpose
Paradigm says it is "very good" because it is the perfect way to
accomplish the Creator's purpose.

A Perishable World

In his first letter to the Corinthian church, Paul makes it clear
that this world was created with a temporary role. Creation was
perishable from the start according to the eternal plan of God, for
God had something better in store—the heavenly city of Hebrews
11:10. This is why the dead in Christ are "sown a perishable body,
[and] it is raised an imperishable body" (1 Corinthians 15:42).
The pattern is clear: first comes the perishable, then comes the
imperishable.

Mortal flesh is identified with the physical world when
Paul writes, "As is the earthy, so also are those who are earthy"
(1 Corinthians 15:48). This temporal, perishable world will give
way to an imperishable world, and the mortal will put on immor-

---

[11] Barnhouse, Donald B., *Commentary on Romans*, Vol 3, "God's Heirs," p.
120.

[12] Morris, Henry, "Old-Earth Creationism," *Back To Genesis*, No. 100a,
April, 1997, The Institute of Creation Research.

tality at the final consummation. From this perspective, decay in the creation indicates a perishable quality inherent from the beginning, not a corruption of nature from the curse. Indeed, this is the anxious longing of all creation that Paul spoke of in Romans 8:19. As the Creator will say in the end, "Behold I am making all things new" (Revelation 21:5).

Suffering Leads to Glory

To properly understand the futility and corruption of creation we must examine the context of Romans 8:19–22. Immediately prior to and immediately after describing the condition of the creation, Paul writes: "For I consider that the sufferings of this present time are not worthy to be compared with the glory that is to be revealed to us. . . . And not only this, but also we ourselves, having the first fruits of the Spirit, even we ourselves groan within ourselves, waiting eagerly for our adoption as sons, the redemption of our body" (Romans 8:18,23). From the context it is clear that the whole creation personifies the child of God in the midst of the Creator's unfolding and eternal plan.

In this passage, futility and corruption directly parallel the temporal suffering, ultimate liberation, and eternal glory that a believer experiences according to the will of God. The central theme running through the context of this passage is that the "sufferings of this present time" are a part of God's eternal plan. Both the material world and the child of God will endure difficulties for a brief time, but the temporal sufferings will give way to eternal glory. Three chapters earlier, Paul established the progression that begins with tribulation and culminates in the hope of God's glory, which he applies here to the entire creation. Paul expresses this same thought to the Corinthians when he writes, "momentary, light affliction is producing for us an eternal weight of glory far beyond all comparison" (2 Corinthians 4:17). This process leads to a predetermined final state and is part of the Master's eternal plan for His creation.

Childbirth is an especially poignant illustration of the Master's plan for creation. Even though the parents know they will suffer, they choose to enter into suffering for a brief, fixed period of time in order to bring about a glorious new life. This is why Paul chose to speak of the whole creation groaning and suffering the pains of childbirth together until the consummation. The whole creation was subjected to the pains of labor by the will of the Father for a time, because it will lead to a glorious new life. This is why Paul prefaced the comment by saying that our sufferings of this present time are not worth comparing to the glory that is to come. This is the correct biblical response to the problem of suffering.

Although we may suffer, the child of God can rest in the sovereignty of God and His plan for our lives. Immediately after describing the futility—and hope—of creation according to the plan of God, Paul encourages the believer to hope in God's plan as well: "And we know that God causes all things to work together for good to those who love God, to those who are called according to His purpose. For whom He foreknew, He also predestined . . . and whom He predestined . . . He also glorified" (Romans 8:28–30).

Here we see what is good from God's perspective. Although it was subjected to futility, the original creation was "very good" because it was created according to God's purpose. His eternal plan is to ultimately work everything together for good as defined by His purpose.

A Better Purpose

The Perfect Purpose Paradigm provides a compelling response to the problem of suffering and evil. Our present sufferings are a part of the fabric of this world as part of the sovereign plan of God. Temporal futility is a necessary part of God's plan through which the rebellion of Satan will be put away and His glory demonstrated. The futility of creation was brought about from the start as part of the bigger picture, "not of its own will, but because of

Him who subjected it in hope" (8:20). Difficulties are part this world, but this world is passing away. Soon the perishable will put on the imperishable, and we will experience the glory God has prepared for His children.

Rather than darkening the heart of a believer, the futility and transience of this life illuminates our longing to be with God. "The sufferings of this present time" make our souls thirst for God "as a deer pants for the water brooks," and we cry out "When shall I come and appear before God?" (Romans 8:18; Psalm 42:1–2). The world was created with innate futility, but at the same time it was imbued with hope. This world is temporary. All of creation is eager for the consummation of God's plan that began before creation. Like a man and woman soon to be married and counting down the days to the consummation of their love, all of creation eagerly awaits the glory that is to come.

This is hope in the genuine biblical sense: it is a longing that is certain to be satisfied. According to the sovereign foreknowledge of God, His predetermined plan was to subject creation to futility in order to accomplish His eternal purpose. In light of the Creator's eternal purpose, an ancient creation with the generations of animal death it entails is fully consistent with His eternal plan.

ANIMAL DEATH AND ATONEMENT

If animal mortality is considered the silver bullet in the age of the earth debate, then the topic of bloodshed and atonement is the gunpowder. This is essentially where the line in the sand is drawn; where the rook card is thrown down to settle the issue. It is the point of contention with the most heat, but not surprisingly, it is also the point with the least light.

Proponents of animal immortality bolster the theological significance of the argument by stating emphatically that if animals died before Adam sinned, then the death of Christ was to no avail. Because of the issue of bloodshed and atonement, proponents of an old earth are said to deny the gospel of salvation. Young earth creationism apologists claim that the very foundation of the gospel message is nullified if animal death occurred apart from the sin of Adam.

The Second Claim:
The Doctrine of Atonement Depends on Original Animal Immortality

Physical death and bloodshed of man and animals came into existence after Adam sinned (Romans 5:12;

1 Corinthians 15). The basis of the Gospel message is that God brought in death and bloodshed because of sin (Hebrews 9:22), so that man could be redeemed. The reason for death is tied up with the message of redemption. . . . In fact, to accept death before man is to destroy the basis of the Gospel message.[1]

If Adam's sin did not bring physical death, Christ's resurrection from physical death does not bring eternal life . . . if death is not the penalty for sin, then the death of Jesus Christ did not pay that penalty, nor did His resurrection from the dead provide eternal life.[2]

The Response

Clearly this is a serious claim that merits examination. Claiming that animal mortality before the fall conflicts with the doctrine of atonement infers that the foundation of our faith depends on original animal immortality. Belief in the gospel supposedly requires believing that there was no animal death prior to the fall. Because the Scriptures do not explicitly teach that animal death came with the curse, this claim can only be defended by theological inference.

Animal Death through Sin

Two passages of Scripture written by Paul are cited as teaching that animal death came about because of man's sin. However, it is readily apparent in both cases that the apostle is specifically and explicitly addressing only human death as a result of man's sin.

---

[1] Ham, Ken, "Billions, Millions, or Thousands: Does It Matter?" *Back To Genesis*, Article No. 29a, The Institute for Creation Research, May 1991.

[2] Morris, John, "Evolution and the Wages of Sin," Impact Article No. 209, The Institute for Creation Research, November, 1990.

The first passage referenced is Romans 5:12–14: "Therefore, just as through one man sin entered into the world, and death through sin, and so death spread to all men, because all sinned—for until the Law sin was in the world; but sin is not imputed when there is no law. Nevertheless death reigned from Adam until Moses, even over those who had not sinned in the likeness of the offense of Adam, who is a type of Him who was to come."

Proponents of the Perfect Paradise Paradigm readily admit that attributing animal mortality to Adam's sin is nothing more than inference from this passage. Commenting on Romans 5:12, it is argued:

> The Bible does indicate that animal death resulted from Adam's sin. . . . True, this verse does emphasize the effect of sin and death upon men, but it does not preclude death from the animal kingdom. "Sin entered the world" could refer only to the world of men (as Dr. Ross suggests), or it could refer to all creation. The context does not directly address this question. It seems likely however, that since other passages of Scripture tell of sin's effect upon nature that this is the intended meaning here as well.[3]

This argument is simply wrong: the context directly addresses the question, and moreover, it disproves the commentator's point. This passage does more than emphasize the effect on man, it explicitly limits the effect to man: "death spread to all men, because all sinned," and death reigned over those who sinned. Sin entered the human race when Adam disobeyed God, and as a result death was visited upon all his descendents. Because animals did not sin, the effect of sin does not spread to them.[4] To include animal death

[3] Van Bebber and Taylor, p. 46.
[4] Munday, p. 58–59.

as a consequence of Adam's transgression is not only unjustified from this passage, it is adding to the Scriptures.

This is quite a rhetorical twist. Proponents initially consider animal death to begin from Adam's sin based on a clear reading of this passage, they then say it is not the emphasis of this passage, and finally they say that it isn't precluded by the text. But to say animal death from sin is not precluded by this passage is at the other end of the spectrum from saying that this passage teaches animal death through sin. They are left to infer the intended meaning.

The second passage used to claim animal mortality entered through the sin of Adam is found in 1 Corinthians 15:21–22, which reads: "For since by a man came death, by a man also came the resurrection of the dead. For as in Adam all die, so also in Christ all shall be made alive" (1 Corinthians 15:21–22).

This text is part of the passage used earlier to describe the eternal plan formulated by God through which all God's enemies are abolished and all authority is subjected to the Father. The context again is referring strictly to the human race. Through the resurrection of Christ, the final enemy, death, will be defeated. The passage states that the ones who die are the same ones who are resurrected and made alive in Christ. If the "all" that die in Adam includes animals, then the "all" made alive by Christ must also include the animals. Certainly this is not the intent of the text since no mention is made in the Scriptures to the spiritual nature of animals, the moral capacity of animals, the need for animal redemption, nor the physical or spiritual resurrection of animals.

Therefore, the two proof texts supposedly linking animal mortality to sin exclusively deal with the impact of sin on man and do not apply to animals. These passages simply cannot be generalized to include the death of animals without disregarding the plain, clear teaching of the passages in order to read a paradigm into the Scriptures.

Atonement through Animal Death

The supposed connection between animal death and the gospel is erroneously derived from the relationship between animal sacrifices in the old covenant with the atoning death of Christ in the new covenant. Ken Ham of *Answers in Genesis*, quoted at the beginning of this chapter, claims that God introduced animal death and bloodshed into the world for the express purpose of redeeming man: "God brought in death and bloodshed . . . so that man could be redeemed." This assertion is simply incorrect. God did not bring in the bloodshed of animals "so that man could be redeemed."

Ham uses Hebrews 9:22 to argue for the connection between animal mortality and the redemption of man based on the necessity of blood for the remission of sins under the old covenant: "And according to the Law, one may almost say, all things are cleansed with blood, and without shedding of blood there is no forgiveness." This passage indicates that God requires a blood payment for sin, without which there is no forgiveness. True, bloodshed is the basis for the gospel, but it is not the shed blood of animals. Hebrews 10:4 makes it clear that animal death cannot redeem, for "it is impossible for the blood of bulls and goats to take away sins." Rather than actually bringing remission of sins, the sacrificial death of particular animals in specific circumstances served as a type of Christ. Those sacrifices did not satisfy the Father; they served as a type of the satisfying payment that was to come. Only the blood of Christ brought ultimate satisfaction to God and redemption to man.

This distinction is often blurred in the context of animal immortality. Speaking of the coats of skin given to Adam and Eve by God after the fall, Ken Ham writes, "God required the shedding of blood for the forgiveness of sins. What happened in the Garden of Eden was a picture what was to come in Jesus Christ, who shed His blood on the Cross as 'the Lamb of God, who takes away the sin of the world,'" (John 1:29). Now if the shedding of blood occurred before sin . . . then the foundation of atonement would be destroyed."⁵

Certainly the provision to Adam and Eve was a picture of Christ's sacrificial death, but that in no way means that the foundation of atonement is destroyed by animal death before the fall. It is only the sacrificial death of animals in the context of levitical law that is related to atonement as a type. Animal death in general is not related to Christ's atonement in any fashion.

Another commentator addresses this spurious linkage of animal mortality to atonement. Commenting on the covering provided to Adam and Eve as well, he writes, "If there was animal death before the fall of man, then God and all those who followed His pattern did useless acts. One must observe that in the atonement the animal loses its life in the place of the human. If animal death existed before the fall, then the object lesson represented by the atoning sacrifice is in reality a cruel joke."⁶

It is sad that such strong language is used to prop up the spurious association between all animal death and atonement. This comment equates all animal death with sacrificial animal death as an atoning substitute for humans. But it is only sacrificial animal death as prescribed by the Law that is associated with atonement. The natural death of an animal has absolutely nothing to do with sacrificial atonement. It was only a particular facet of animal death that was an object lesson—a type of Christ—and one that certainly was not rendered a "cruel joke" by pre-fall animal mortality. It is simply incorrect to identify all animal death with animal sacrifice in the context of atonement.

⁵ Ham, Ken, "What Really Happened to the Dinosaurs?" *Answers in Genesis*, 2001, p. 39.

⁶ Stambaugh, James, "Death Before Sin?" ICR Impact No. 191, May 1989.

Focal Points

The atoning death of Christ is not affected by the death of animals prior to the fall of Adam. The death of animals prior to man's sin does not alter the consequences of sin nor render its atonement meaningless. The Bible states that sin brought death to man. The death of an animal in relation to atonement only has meaning as a picture of the death of God's only Son. Clearly the death of animals is not a necessary element of atonement but is only a type, pointing to the death of Christ. The principle of Ham and Morris is not correct—the basis of the gospel is not that God "brought in death and bloodshed (of animals) . . . so that man could be redeemed." God used the sacrificial death of animals as a picture to illustrate the Redeemer, the only Lamb of God who would take away the sins of the world. This, not animal death, is the basis of the gospel.

ANIMAL DEATH IN
A "VERY GOOD" WORLD

According to the Perfect Paradise Paradigm, when God said "very good" He said a mouthful. Proponents of the Perfect Paradise Paradigm believe that from God's perspective a "very good" creation could not possibly include animal death. Essentially, animal death before sin is assumed to be inconsistent with the nature of God. One of the most appealing arguments against animal death before the fall is that God simply would not have considered that to be "very good."

The Third Claim:
Animal Death and Suffering Could Not Be Considered "Very Good" by a Loving, Wise, and Merciful Creator.

The main point is that death, bloodshed, and suffering of living creatures were not possible before the fall. It was a perfect world. . . .[1]

---

[1] Ham, Ken, "Adam and the Ants," *Back To Genesis*, No. 33a, September 1991, The Institute of Creation Research.

To us literal creationists, on the other hand, it seems unthinkable that the God of the Bible—the God who is omniscient and omnipotent, merciful and loving— would do anything like that (allow animal death before creating Adam). Surely He could devise a better plan than this.[2]

There was, therefore, nothing bad in that created world, no hunger, no struggle for existence, no suffering, and certainly no death of animal or human life anywhere in God's perfect creation.[3]

. . . The completed creation was "very good" (Genesis 1:31), with nothing bad or unfair or hurtful—certainly no "struggle for existence" or "survival of the fittest," or any lack of anything needed by any of God's created beings or systems.[4]

Which type of world could God call "very good?" All Christian advocates of an old earth must hold that Sue (a Tyrannosaurus Rex skeleton), her time, and condition predated Adam, and thus was deemed "very good" by God. . . . Surely some things just can't be.[5]

---

[2] Morris, Henry, "Old-Earth Creationism," *Back To Genesis*, No. 100a, April, 1997, The Institute of Creation Research.

[3] Morris, Henry, "The Fall, The Curse, and Evolution," *Back To Genesis*, No. 112a, April, 1998, The Institute of Creation Research.

[4] Morris, Henry, "The Finished Works of God," *Back To Genesis*, No. 136a, April, 2000, The Institute of Creation Research.

[5] Morris, John, *Acts and Facts*, January 2002, The Institute of Creation Research.

The Response

"Very good" is the point of departure between the two creation paradigms. The entire Perfect Paradise Paradigm is derived from the presumption that by these two words God meant absolute perfection. As if He were required to demonstrate the extreme perfection of His creative ability, anything less than utter perfection is deemed to be beneath Him. Although it is perhaps a common idyllic notion, this purely sentimental perspective does not accord with the Scriptures.

When God called the creation "very good," He did not mean that the world was absolutely perfect in every imaginable way. The world was "very good" in a particular, specific way. Because the world was perfectly suited, by design, to the execution of His perfect plan and the accomplishment of His eternal purpose, the Creator called it "very good." Revelation 4:11 provides the key insight to what God meant by a "very good" creation. According to the twenty-four elders around the throne of God, everything that God created brings Him pleasure because it brings Him glory through the execution of His plan. Thus the creation was "very good" based on the utility of the physical universe for accomplishing its purpose for existence. Just as the child of God is His workmanship, created in Christ Jesus for good works (Ephesians 2:10), all of creation was sculpted to accomplish a task. It was perfect from God's perspective and the purpose for which it was created.

Because God is immutable, and His plan is eternal, His ultimate end is always in view. Something considered "very good" by God must be "very good" in light of His ultimate end for it. Creation's goodness did not preclude the fall—it included the totality of history. The Creator did not cross His fingers, put on blinders and say "Okay, this is very good, now please don't mess it up!" When God called His creation "very good" it was in the full knowledge of the events to come. Creation was "very good" in light of its ultimate end: the perfect purpose of God.

A "Very Good" Creation

After creating the heavens and the earth and all that is in them, God called His completed work of creation "very good" (Genesis 1:31). The created world could be nothing less since it was created according to the good purpose of God, "for everything created by God is good" (1 Timothy 4:4).[6]

The choice of wording demonstrates that the goodness of creation should be viewed from a perspective of utility rather than sheer perfection. The Hebrew phrase translated "very good" in Genesis 1:31 is *meod tob*, where *tob* is translated at various places as "pleasing," "blameless," or "what seems best." Other Hebrew words could have been used if the intent was absolute perfection, but instead God chose to use wording that more generally describes a quality of beauty or a fitness for a purpose. The same phrase is used in Genesis 24:16 where Rebekah is said to be *meod tob*, or "very beautiful." Joshua and Caleb reported back to the people of Israel that the Promised Land was *meod tob*, or "exceedingly good" (Numbers 14:7). Neither Rebekah nor the Promised Land was perfect in every way, but both were exactly right for the purpose.

The original creation is not the only thing that God considers to be good. Recall the ordeal that Joseph had gone through on his way to becoming the second in command in Egypt. He had been sold into slavery by his brothers, falsely charged and convicted by his boss's wife, and forsaken by his fellow captives. None of this suffering came about because of Joseph's disobedience but rather by the hand of God. When he revealed his identity to his

---

[6] Christian philosophers have long argued that "very good" does not imply perfection of the creation in the same sense that God is perfect. Liebnitz argued that only God is completely perfect and the creation must be less than the Creator. Unlike the incorruptible Creator (Romans 1:23), the finite creation is susceptible to corruption. Otherwise, if the creation were morally pure and perfect in the same sense as the Creator, the earth and humanity would not even be susceptible to sin.

brothers, they were rightly afraid. But Joseph told them that even though they intended to hurt him, God intended it for good (*tob*). Although young earth creationism apologists claim that *tob* "never refers to something that hurts"[7] Joseph illustrates the error in this view. The Bible clearly teaches that God used difficulties in the life of Joseph to bring about a greater good.

Several hundred years later when the time came for God to deliver His people out of bondage in Egypt, He promised to "bring them out to a good and spacious land" (Exodus 3:8). But this land that God called good was not without suffering or difficulties. Although it was "a land flowing with milk and honey," it was also "the place of the Canaanite and the Hittite and the Amorite and the Perizzite and the Hivite and the Jebusite." To gain the blessings of the Promised Land they first had to subdue the occupants. This was certainly not a land of absolute perfection, but God called it good nonetheless. Here again we see something God considers good because it was fitting for His eternal purpose during human history.

Perhaps the most poignant example of what God considers good is Jesus Himself. Isaiah prophesied about the sufferings and sacrificial death of the Savior, saying "the Lord was pleased to crush Him, putting Him to grief; if He would render Himself as a guilt offering" (Isaiah 53:10). The cross is the ultimate example of suffering that brings Him pleasure because it is consistent with His eternal plan. The cross is also the ultimate rebuttal against the claim that a loving and powerful God would prevent all suffering and evil. The same God who chose not to prevent suffering and evil did a greater thing—He entered creation and overcame evil through His own suffering.

In fact, nowhere is *meod tob* interpreted as absolute perfection other than Genesis 1:31, and in that case it is for sentimental rather

---

[7] Morris, Henry, III, *After Eden*, Master Books, 2003, p. 104.

than exegetical reasons. Giving testimony to this fact is a leading proponent of the Perfect Paradise Paradigm who writes: "it seems unthinkable that the God of the Bible—the God who is omniscient and omnipotent, merciful and loving—would do anything like that (allow animal death before the fall). Surely He could devise and implement a better plan that this." [8]

Notice the identification of animal mortality with the larger problem of suffering and evil. Young earth creationism believes a loving God could devise a better plan than this. But this is to define what God's plan could be by what seems thinkable to us. If we think it could have been better, then surely it must have been better. A major contributor to the disdain for the possibility of an old earth is this sentimental and subjective view of animal death. "Progressive creationists see no theological or Biblical problems with having animal death prior to human sin, nor in the idea of billions of animals suffering and dying long before God got around to placing them under man's dominion. . . . We literal creationists do see problems in this idea, however. The concept of an omnipotent, omniscient, loving, caring God devising such a scheme somehow seems to stick in our mental throats whenever they ask us to swallow it."[9]

Perhaps the difficulty with the notion of an ancient earth illustrates how God's ways are higher than our ways, and His thoughts are higher than our thoughts. This is exactly the error of Peter when he thought He knew God's plan better than Jesus. Peter thought that the death of Jesus would be a great evil—surely He misunderstood God's plan. Certainly the notion of Jesus being killed stuck in Peter's mental throat, and he could not swallow it.

---

[8] Morris, Henry, "The Fall, the Curse, and Evolution," *Back To Genesis*, No. 112a, The Institute for Creation Research, April 1998.

[9] Morris, Henry, "The Wolf and the Lamb," *Back To Genesis*, No. 69a, The Institute for Creation Research, September 1994.

But as we know from the rebuke of Jesus, it was Peter who was putting His thoughts ahead of the plan of God. The point is simply this, we must be cautious when our theology is based on what seems unthinkable or what seems to us to be a better plan.

Imago Dei

Perhaps people err on the topic of animal death before the fall because they fail to recognize the distinction between man and animal in the economy of God's creation. From the perspective of the Perfect Paradise Paradigm, God would never have called the world He created "very good" if it included animal death. However, the Scriptures teach that that God views the death of man very differently from the death of animals. Those who claim that animal death is incompatible with the nature of God fail to recognize the reason that man is unique and distinct from animals: he alone is created in God's image.

There is a fundamental difference in the death of animals and the death of man because of the unique position of humans in the created order. Immediately after giving Noah permission to kill animals for food (Genesis 9:4), God said that He would require justice "from every beast . . . that sheds man's blood" (Genesis 9:5–6). But the converse is not true—God does not require the lifeblood of someone who takes the life of an animal. God gives a prohibition against murder in the very passage where man is given permission to kill animals for food. The basis for the distinction is that the blood of man is special, "for in the image of God He made man" (Genesis 9:6). God does not prohibit the killing of animals because there is simply no equivalence between the death of animals and the death of man. Only man is uniquely created in the image of God.

"Very Good" after the Fall

Based on the immutability of God's nature and the eternal singularity of His purpose, the fall could not have changed what God considers good. It follows that if He considered something to be good after the fall, then it must have also been good before the fall. In other words, the fall did not change what the Creator considers "very good." Yet in several instances, the Bible speaks of God considering something to be good that is inconsistent with the notion of a Perfect Paradise. In particular, if all animal death was bad before the fall, then it was not made good by the fall.

Far from tainting the character of God, the Bible clearly asserts that animal death is part of the Creator's plan to accomplish His eternal purpose. God uses the death of animals for His glory and calls it good.

Predator and Prey

My daughter went on a field trip with her first grade class to a local nature trail. One of the games they played helped them learn about food sources. She learned how the sun feeds a flower, how a flower feeds a grasshopper, how a grasshopper feeds a frog, how a frog feeds a snake, how a snake feeds an owl, and so on. This was a wonderful object lesson on the Creator's wisdom and providential care manifested in the balance of nature. Animal death is an undeniably necessary part of nature. Any other scenario would be a completely different natural world. The problem for the Perfect Paradise Paradigm is that God says He created this present natural order for His purpose and that it declares His glory.

This is affirmed in Scripture, for God declares through Isaiah that the predator and the prey accomplish His purposes:

> I am God, and there is no one like Me,
> Declaring the end from the beginning,
> And from ancient times things which have not been done,
> Saying, "My purpose will be established,

And I will accomplish all My good pleasure;"
Calling a bird of prey from the east. . . .
I have planned it, surely I will do it. (Isaiah 46:9–11)

Here we have an Old Testament reference to the eternal plan of God. Demonstrating that He alone is God, the Creator declares both beginning and end. His purpose will be established and His good pleasure accomplished. What example is given of accomplishing His "good pleasure?" What demonstrates the establishment of His "purpose?" God uses a bird of prey.

Another very interesting example of what God considers good is found in Psalm 104:24–28. The Psalmist points out Leviathan, which God created to "sport" in the seas. The passage praises God for His wisdom and providential care over all of His creation. All creatures great and small depend on God for sustenance; "they all wait for you to give them their food in due season" (Psalm 104:27). It is God's hand that provides for their needs, and they are satisfied with "good" (*tob*). This concept runs directly across the grain of the Perfect Paradise Paradigm but is a biblical certainty. God says that His provision of prey for the predator is good.[10]

Breaking Paradigms with a Whirlwind

The notion that there was a paradise with no animal suffering or death before the fall would have been foreign to Job after He sat in silence while God spoke from the whirlwind. The examples God provided to Job are particularly relevant to this topic because in many cases, the Creator's case studies exhibit characteristics that are inconsistent with the young earth creationism view of what "very good" means. God does not explain these characteristics as a result of the fall but rather uses them to illustrate His wisdom and glorious, sovereign power!

---

[10] See also Hugh Ross, *A Matter of Days*, NavPress, 2004, p. 102.

Hungry Young Lions. With example after example, God demonstrates His providence to Job through meeting the needs of carnivorous animals.

> Can you hunt the prey for the lion,
> Or satisfy the appetite of the young lions,
> When they crouch in their dens
> And lie in wait in their lair?
> Who prepares for the raven its nourishment
> When its young cry to God
> And wander about without food? (Job 38:39–41)

God provides food to satisfy the appetite of the young lions that lie in wait for their prey (also stated in Psalm 104:21). He prepares food for the raven when its young cry out to Him in hunger. God does not denounce predation or indicate that He would rather have it another way, but simply states that He provides food for the predator. Far from rendering the Creator cruel and sadistic, the predator and their prey illustrate His sovereign power and accomplish His purpose.

Cruel Mother Ostrich. God uses things for His glory according to His eternal plan that the Perfect Paradise Paradigm would conclude occurred only after the fall. Yet God doesn't excuse His behavior by blaming it on sin. Having no part in sin and no shadow of unrighteousness, God points out parts of His creation doing His bidding that are in conflict with the Perfect Paradise Paradigm. Another interesting example of this principle is found in Job 39:13–17, where God points out the ostrich as a demonstration of His sovereign wisdom.

> The ostriches' wings flap joyously
>   With the pinion and plumage of love,
> For she abandons her eggs to the earth
>   And warms them in the dust,
> And she forgets that a foot may crush them,
>   Or that a wild beast may trample them.

> She treats her young cruelly, as if they were not hers;
> Though her labor be in vain, she is unconcerned;
> Because God has made her forget wisdom,
> And has not given her a share of understanding.

Describing the ostrich, God says, "she abandons her eggs" and "treats her young cruelly." Some would argue that this cruelty in nature is inconsistent with a "very good" creation and must be the result of the curse pronounced on creation after the fall of Adam. But that is not the case. The reason the ostrich acts cruelly toward her young is "because God has made her to forget wisdom and has not given her a share of understanding." Note that blame is not placed on the curse, the fall, or the flood. The Creator takes credit for the seemingly cruel behavior in the animal kingdom in order to demonstrate His sovereign control and provision over all creation. This is an excellent counter-example to the Perfect Paradise Paradigm from the animal kingdom. Predation and apparent cruelty in nature are part of God's original plan and not a result of the curse. Predation is "very good" in light of the eternal purpose of God.

Eagle Eyes. Just after describing the ostrich, God gives another counter-example to the false premise of the Perfect Paradise Paradigm. In verses 27 to 30, God describes His provision for the eagle:

> Is it at your command that the eagle mounts up
> And makes his nest on high?
> On the cliff he dwells and lodges,
> Upon the rocky crag, an inaccessible place.
> From there he spies out food;
> His eyes see it from afar.
> His young ones also suck up blood;
> And where the slain are, there is he.

The answer to this rhetorical question is clear. God is the one who commands the eagle to make a nest on high. He is the one who provides food for the young eagles. But the food He provides is bloody. These carnivores eat the flesh of slain animals, all by the command of God. Certainly God would not command animals to behave in a way that is contrary to His nature and point to it as an example of His glory. The clear implication is that the natural order of predator and prey is part of the eternal plan of God and not a result of the curse. The Bible demonstrates the truth that animal predation is part of God's provision for creation.

VEGETARIAN DELIGHT 15

In the previous chapters, three arguments for animal immortality have been considered. First, the curse was examined to show that animal death was not introduced as a penalty on the animal kingdom for the sin of Adam. Second, although the rhetoric would imply otherwise, the atonement secured through the death of Christ is not affected by animal death before the fall. And third, when God described the world as "very good," it did not imply that there was no death in the animal kingdom. In this chapter, the final argument advanced to prove that there was no animal death before the fall is considered.

The Fourth Claim:
All Animals Were Created as Herbivores and Commanded To Be Vegetarians.

In brief, this verse (Genesis 1:30) is an indication of the perfect harmony prevailing in the animal world. No beast preyed upon the other. Rapacious and ferocious wild beasts did not yet exist. This verse, then, indicates very briefly for this chapter what is unfolded at length in chapter two, that a paradise-like state prevailed at creation.[1]

Originally, before sin, *all* animals, including dinosaurs, were vegetarian.[2]

God said very clearly that both man and animals were only to eat plants, in Genesis 1:29.[3]

The Response

As if to ensure that predatory behavior in the animal kingdom would not be tolerated, the claim is made that before the fall God commanded both man and animals to only eat vegetation. But is it correct that "God said very clearly that both man and animals were *only* to eat plants?" At first glance, this seems to be a strong argument against animal death prior to the fall. After all, if God said very clearly that animals were only to eat plants, then the issue should be settled. However, upon scrutiny, this argument loses its appeal. In fact, God did not command all animals to be vegetarians.

A Bountiful Provision

The creation narrative is a focused account of the man and woman specially crafted in God's image and their interaction with the Creator and His creation. In this inerrant historical narrative, we see God using the created world to show Adam His power, His providence, and His provision. Because it is characterized by brevity, we must be diligent to understand the meaning of the text while being careful not to interpret it too narrowly nor press it

---

[1] Morris, Henry, *The Genesis Flood*, p. 463.

[2] Ham, Ken, *What Really Happened to Dinosaurs (Booklet)*, Answers in Genesis, 2001, p. 20 (emphasis in original).

[3] Stambaugh, James, "Death Before Sin?" Impact Article No. 191, May 1989, The Institute for Creation Research.

for a meaning that was not intended. The creation account is not an exhaustive inventory of everything God created. Nor is it a comprehensive description of the functions and characteristics of everything God created. The text is not concerned with the mating habits of the arctic tern because that isn't pertinent to the topic at hand. Neither is the diet of animals the point of this passage.

After finishing His work of creation, God gave Adam a personal tour of the Garden, pointing out the lavish beauty of the Garden and the abundant provision He had made for Adam's every need. "Then God said, 'Behold, I have given you every plant yielding seed that is on the surface of all the earth, and every tree which has fruit yielding seed; it shall be food for you; and to every beast of the earth and to every bird of the sky and to every thing that moves on the earth which has life, I have given every green plant for food;' and it was so," (Genesis 1:29–30).

There are several reasons why this passage should not be understood as an indication that all animals were herbivores. Most importantly, this narrow view detracts from the rich theological significance of the text. Like the proverbial glass of water, this is a passage that can be seen as either half-full or half-empty. Young earth creationism apologists see this in a negative sense as a restriction on Adam's liberty, as if God had literally given every green plant for food, but nothing else. Taken in a positive sense, it is an indication of the rich provision God had given His creation.

A Singular Prohibition

God allowed freedom for Adam to explore the creation and learn about the Creator. The Garden of Eden was a special place where God's gracious provision abounded in every way. It was a place specially suited and amply stocked for its favored inhabitants. In the midst of Adam's wide range of moral freedom, God gave him only one restriction.

Rather than narrowly interpreting this passage simply as a restriction, it should be seen as a positive indication of God's provision to man. In essence God said to Adam, "Look at the incredible richness of my gracious provision for you. I have provided every fruit and vegetable that you could possibly want. There is more than enough here for you and the animals. Nothing I have created has any want or is lacking in any way. Obey me and I will provide you a rich and full life. All I require is this one thing: do not eat from that tree." The reason God explicitly told Adam "I have given every green plant for food" was not to limit his diet; it was to contrast the bountiful provision with the singular prohibition. Adam had no excuse to disobey.

Pointing out the range of freedom is not the same as restricting the range of freedom. Young earth creationism presses the Scripture too far on this point. God did not say, "You must only eat green plants." What He said was simply, "I have given every green plant for food." Food is specifically mentioned because the medium for moral instruction and testing was fruit. Life and death depended on the fruit from two trees. Because the prohibition was related to fruit, God first made it clear to Adam that he had plenty of delicious fruits and vegetables of all kinds to satisfy his appetite. The intent was to emphasize the ample provision in contrast to the single prohibition.

A Silent Command

We must be very careful inferring commands from silence. Only one aspect of Adam's diet rose to the level of a moral command—he was not permitted to eat from the Tree of Knowledge. God explicitly told Adam that there was only one tree from which he was not allowed to eat, and the consequences for disobedience were explicit and clear. Aside from that, there is no prohibition of any type anywhere else in the text. To infer a command against eating meat essentially adds a second restriction in addition to the Tree of Knowledge. There was only one commandment given to Adam, and that was a single dietary commandment to not eat from a particular tree.

Animals were in no way restricted from eating from the Tree of Life or from the Tree of the Knowledge of Good and Evil. Animals were mentioned so that Adam would know God had amply provided enough for all of the garden's inhabitants. Ackland correctly observes that "the beast of the field and the fowl of the air were to be co-proprietors with him; they were to have the use of it as freely as himself; but that they were to be restricted to the use of vegetable food nowhere appears."[4]

Pots and Pans at Grandma's House

My young children love to play in the kitchen at their grandparents' house. Their grandmother keeps a collection of plastic bowls and cups of all shapes, sizes, and colors in a kitchen cabinet, just for the grandkids to take out for play. When she begins boiling a pot of noodles while the children are playing in the kitchen (macaroni and cheese is the staple of their diet) she says to them, "Now kids, you can play with any of the bowls in this cabinet, but do no touch the pot on the stove. If you do, it will burn you." Even though the pot on the stove holds their beloved macaroni—it may not make one wise, but it is appealing to the eyes and good tasting—they are strictly and clearly prohibited from touching it. They are given more than enough containers to play with. They are not lacking or deprived of any good thing by their Grandmother's restriction. They have no excuse to disobey. This is like the bountiful provision given to Adam and Eve.

But this illustration goes further. When Grandma tells the kids that they can play with any pot or bowl in the kitchen, does she mean that they can only play with the kitchen containers? Do the kids think it is wrong to go play with a puzzle in the bedroom? Are the coloring books off limits? Are they disobedient if they go outside to play with the swing? No, the provision and the prohibi-

---

[4] Ackland, T. S., "The Story of Creation as told by Theology and by Science," London, Society for Promoting Christian Knowledge, 1890.

tion are clear. "I've given you plenty of pots to play with, so don't touch this one." Like a good parent, God provides for His children and makes His prohibitions clear. The boundaries are explicit, and the freedom within is complete.

Permission to Eat Meat

Apparently God did intend for Adam to be a vegetarian, but that is not indicated until the ninth chapter of Genesis where we find the first reference to eating meat. After the flood, God explicitly states that man is permitted to eat meat. "Every moving thing that is alive shall be food for you; I give all to you, as I gave the green plant. Only you shall not eat flesh with its life, that is, its blood. Surely I will require your lifeblood; from every beast I will require it. And from every man, from every man's brother I will require the life of man. Whoever sheds man's blood, by man his blood shall be shed, for in the image of God He made man" (Genesis 9:3–6).

There is a structural tie between these two passages through the tense of the text. God tells Noah that he is now given "every moving thing that is alive" for food, "as I gave the green plant," in reference to Genesis 1:29. Noah was given permission to eat meat just as Adam had been given provision with the green plants. Clearly absent from the Genesis 9 text is a reference to the diet of animals, even though the animals are specifically mentioned in Genesis 1:29. The permission given to Noah does not imply a previous restriction on the animals. Rather, the absence of animal diets in Genesis 9 indicates that the focus of the dietary instructions in Genesis 1 is strictly on man.[5] Instead of proving that animals did not eat meat, this text suggests that the diet of animals is not the point of Genesis 1:29.

---

[5] MacDonald, p. 390.

Genesis 9:3–6 actually implies that animals were permitted to eat meat before the fall. Otherwise there is no mention made as to when God would have allowed animals to eat meat. This distinction is important; if one assumes that the permission for man in Genesis 9:3 implies a prohibition for man in Genesis 1:29, then the absence of permission for animals in Genesis 9:3 must indicate the absence of a prohibition on animals in Genesis 1:29. The absence of permission for animals to eat meat in any place indicates that there were no dietary restrictions on animals before the flood or the fall.

Of course God did not have to record in Scripture when He removed the limitation. One suggestion is that animals became carnivores as part of the curse, but the timing is inconsistent with God's permission for man after the flood. Perhaps man was only permitted to eat meat after the flood in order to promote his health. This would also permit the harmony between man and animals that would be necessary to coexist on the ark. But harmony would be just as beneficial between animals on the ark. The predators could be separated from the prey on the ark, but consistency would imply that animal predation would be deferred until after the flood as well. Since animal immortality proponents attribute the biological changes made to herbivores to the environmental changes after the flood, it would seem even more consistent to assign those changes after the flood. If Genesis 1:29 were in fact a dietary command to the animals, consistency with Genesis 9:3–6 implies that God would have also mentioned if animal diets changed either after the fall or after the flood. Hence one is left to conclude that animal diets have always been the same as they were originally created to be.

Distinct from the Animals

It is erroneous to consider God's dealings with the animals the same as His dealings with Adam. This obvious distinction between man and animal is made explicit in 1 Corinthians 15:39, which says, "All flesh is not the same flesh, but there is one flesh of men, and another flesh of beasts, and another flesh of birds, and another of fish." Through this discourse, Paul highlights the significant distinction between Adam and the animals. Man was uniquely created in the image of God, with a moral capacity and moral accountability. That distinction is essential to understand the dietary statements from God to Adam.

In the first chapter of Genesis, God describes the bounty of His provision and Adam's liberty to enjoy the sustenance of God. The restriction placed on Adam doesn't come until the second chapter. To paraphrase once again, God said, "See Adam, I've given you and the animals the freedom to eat from any tree or plant in the garden (chapter 1). But Adam, you are different from the animals. You must not eat from this one tree (chapter 2)." A distinction is drawn between Adam and the animals, namely the animals were not given any restrictions. Both the prohibition and the provision are specifically directed to Adam and only incidentally to animals. He alone was a moral creature who related to God in a unique way. God made it clear that the provision for physical nourishment was sufficient for both man and animal, but Adam also was created with a spirit in need of nourishment.

God interacted with Adam in a unique way because Adam was uniquely created in the image of God. Adam had a spiritual hunger that was satisfied only through communion with the Creator. Adam was different from the animals because he had a moral capacity. His moral capacity and devotion to the Creator was put to test by one single restriction in the midst of liberty and bounty. Adam's diet was restricted on a moral basis, not because of anything inherently unseemly with eating meat. Because the animals had no moral capacity and no spiritual communion with the Creator, the same basis for restricting their diet did not exist.

For the animals, there was no possible blessing from the Tree of Life nor was there any restriction from the Tree of Knowledge. It is like comparing apples and oranges to infer that God's statement of provision was an inferred limitation on the animals. The only dietary prohibition was against eating from the single tree, and it was addressed only to Adam.

Every Plant Edible

Genesis 1:29 and 30 draws a clear distinction between the provision to man and to the animals. Adam is given "every plant yielding seed . . . and every tree which has fruit yielding seed," while the animals are given "every green plant." As if every animal could eat every plant, a more extensive diet is given to the animals. According to Dawson, "this cannot mean that every animal in the earth was herbivorous. It may refer to the group of animals associated with man in Eden, and this is most likely the intention of the writer; but if it includes the animals of the whole earth, we may be certain . . . that it indicates the general fact that the whole animal kingdom is based on vegetation."[6] This would then be a reference to the general fact that even strictly carnivorous animals are indirectly dependent on green plants as nourishment for their prey. Kidner points out that "the assignment of 'every green plant for food' to all creatures must not be pressed to mean that all were once herbivorous, any more than to mean that all plants were equally edible to all. It is a generalization, that directly or indirectly all life depends on vegetation, and the concern of the verse is to show that all are fed from God's hand."[7] Perhaps God was not only revealing to Adam His gracious means of provision for all life but also showing Adam the significance of his duty to cultivate and keep the earth since all life depended on the fruit of the ground.

[6] Dawson, p. 240–241.
[7] Kidner, p. 52.

Focal Points

The implication is clear. The singular moral prohibition to Adam was a dietary restriction from a single tree. Animals are not moral creatures and hence had no moral restrictions placed upon them. They could have eaten freely from the forbidden tree without consequence. Likewise they could have eaten from the Tree of Life without its consequent blessings. Neither tree was intended for them. The intention of the Creator was not to prohibit or proscribe the diets of animals; it was to establish a context of bounty for man's singular prohibition.

TRUTH OR CONSEQUENCES 16

My collision with Dr. McLynn was not my first encounter with her worldview; for most of my life I had ascribed to it as well. As a young Christian fascinated with science, I had a strong hunger to learn about creation. I attended seminars, listened to tapes, watched videos, and voraciously read every book I could find that dealt with scientific creationism. I prepared myself for battle and was ready to take on the evolutionists who were conspiring to destroy my faith.

Armed with an arsenal of young earth creationism arguments, I set out to expose the evolutionists' dirty little secret that the earth is young and the fact that they knew it.[1] It was not until I actually tried to use my weapons that I realized they were ineffective. What happened next was nothing less than a tectonic shift in my worldview.

---

[1] Again the premise is that since vast amounts of time are required for evolution, a young earth is a divinely created earth. This perspective fails to account for the fact that evolution is distinct from time and that not even vast amounts of time suffice for the naturalistic evolution of life on earth.

A Train Wreck

As a doctoral candidate in my late twenties, I was eager to engage my secular colleagues about evolution and the Christian faith. We enthusiastically discussed the problems of abiogenesis (the origination of life from nonliving matter), the sparsity of the fossil record, and the information content of DNA. But when it came to the age of the earth, I was in for a great surprise. My colleagues graciously showed me the flaws in my "scientific evidence." Essentially my arguments were either based on obsolete data, an incomplete understanding of the processes, or mere speculation. Even more surprising was the overwhelming wealth of evidence for an old earth that I was unaware of. While my creationist leaders had done an excellent job bringing to light the insurmountable problems with naturalistic biological evolution, the unavoidable conclusion was that I was not fully informed about the age of the earth.

Naturally, I wondered what this meant for all the biblical arguments for a young earth. I fully believed that the truth of Scripture was not to be subjected to a secular arbiter, but I also believed that it would always line up on the side of truth. I was convinced that if the Bible indeed taught that the earth was young, then there had to be a problem with science. But in this case, the strength of the evidence suggested that the problem had to lie with what I thought the Bible taught.

So I reasoned that if I did not know the complete story on the science of creation, maybe there was also more to learn on the biblical side. Again to my surprise I learned that indeed there are valid interpretations of the Genesis days other than strict 24-hour calendar days. It turns out that many conservative, reputable Bible scholars and linguists argue from the Bible itself that the days must have been ages of time.[2] While many Christians throughout

---

[2] See footnote 4, Part 1.

the church age have held to a 24-hour view, there have always been many who considered the length of the days an open question.[3] Even as early as the fourth century, the early church father Augustine wrote in *The City of God* XI, 6, "What kind of days these were it is extremely difficult, or perhaps impossible for us to conceive . . ." Like many without insight from modern science, Augustine recognized that there is latitude of meaning with the days of creation. The issue had never been as certain as I had been taught.

A huge weight was lifted from my shoulders when I realized that an ancient creation did not violate biblical inerrancy, the historical truth of Genesis, or sound theology. My brain cramp was gone. For the first time in my life I had a consistent and defensible worldview that integrated God's great truth revealed in His word and His world. With one consistent story, the heavens tell of His glory (Psalm 19:1–2) and the Scriptures tell of His Son (John 5:39). Rather than ignoring the dilemma of faith backed by wishful thinking and opposed by common knowledge, I became convinced that what I believed was reasonable both biblically and scientifically.

On the Cusp of Discovery

This is a great time to be a Bible-believing creationist. Never before have the "invisible attributes" of the Creator been more clearly seen in the natural world (Romans 1:20). Every day scientists are further confirming that the universe and the laws of nature appear to be precisely tuned according to a grand design. The (geologically) abrupt appearance of complex life on earth

---

[3] An excellent nonpartisan treatment of the history on the creation date controversy is the *Report of the Creation Study Committee*, published in 2000 by the Administrative Committee, Presbyterian Church in America,1852 Century Place, Suite 190, Atlanta, GA 30345.

gives every indication of special creation by the One who said "let there be!" The rich information content found in even the simplest forms of life cries out for an intelligent source. George Greenstein, an agnostic physicist, stated it well when he said, "As we survey all the evidence, the thought insistently arises that some supernatural agency—or, rather, Agency—must be involved. Is it possible that suddenly, without intending to, we have stumbled upon scientific proof of the existence of a Supreme Being? Was it God who stepped in and so providentially crafted the cosmos for our benefit?"[4] When the evidence is examined, the conclusion is hard to miss: the heavens, the earth, and life itself are the products of a purposeful Designer.

There is no reason for a Christian to fear the discoveries of science that wait around the corner. There is no need to rely on superficial science and anecdotal speculation to support our biblical faith and worldview. We are on the cusp of even greater discoveries to affirm our faith and help us destroy "speculations and every lofty thing raised up against the knowledge of God" (2 Corinthians 10:5).

So now my faith is continually affirmed by the amassing evidence for the Creator's handiwork in the heavens and in my heart. But is it enough that I settled the issue? Should it matter that the conflict remains for others? No significant damage was done by my worldview crisis, but unfortunately this is not always the case.

Double Jeopardy

There will always be an abundance of issues to wrestle with in the family of God. Many of the things that divide us are not worth

---

[4] Greenstein, George, *Symbiotic Universe,* William Morrow and Company, 1988, p. 27.

fighting for, but the impact of some issues is felt far beyond the church doors. How the church deals with the time of creation is often more important on Monday than it is on Sunday. Pastors and Christian leaders throughout the land must come to recognize the importance of this issue. Exactly why the age of the earth matters is a case of double jeopardy.

Jeopardizing Faith

A great emphasis should be placed on the centrality of Genesis to the major doctrines of the Bible. In the first three chapters we learn much about the nature of the Creator, the origin of sin and human death, and the Redeemer's foreshadowed provision for that sin. Yet many who rightly emphasize the foundational significance of Genesis also equate those foundational doctrines with the young earth creation worldview. To many sincere pastors and bible students, the great doctrines of the Creator, sin, and redemption are inseparably bound up with a recent creation.

Inseparably linking the Perfect Paradise Paradigm to the heart of Christian doctrine and biblical authority is more than incorrect, it is potentially devastating. It is vitally important to teach our children that the Christian faith is objectively true and defensible. Science is not the final answer; certainly we must teach them to question the presumptions and conclusions of scientists. But if we dogmatically assert a simplistic and erroneous defense of our faith, then the substantive truth of our faith is marginalized and our children are at risk. If our children learn that we err on these matters, why would they believe us when we teach them of the death and resurrection of Christ?

When we fail to prepare our youth with the solid foundation of a credible Christian worldview, we risk losing them to the secular society. The simple fact is that our young people are misled when they are taught that the scientific evidence for an ancient creation is not credible. How will they react when they learn that the evidence points to one answer and it is not what they had been taught? When they are confronted with the incompleteness and inaccuracies on which their creation world-view was established, the faith built on that foundation will be in jeopardy. If they come to think that the Bible is wrong in the first three chapters, they will likely reject the rest as well.

Jeopardizing the Great Commission

There is also a risk for those who do not yet believe. Scripture admonishes us to not add anything to the gospel that might encumber or prevent someone from coming to the truth. We are not to add a burdensome yoke to their back as they seek the Savior. When the age of the earth is raised to the level of orthodoxy and inseparably bound up with the core doctrines of the Christian faith, we run the risk of doing just this.

More importantly, placing the age of the earth at the heart of our doctrines discredits the authority of Scripture. Certainly a person who is not a follower of Christ is blind to spiritual truth until the Spirit of God quickens them to the truth in Scripture. But there are clearly many matters of common knowledge outside the Bible that do not require the Spirit's intervention to understand. When Christians appeal to seekers and skeptics with a worldview that is contrary to common knowledge, we risk marginalizing the very truth on which their souls depend. This is a grave danger. Augustine astutely observes that it will bring shame and derision for a Christian to be heard speaking erroneously from the Scriptures about a matter of common knowledge. But more importantly, Augustine charges that the real evil is that the unbeliever will think that the Bible itself is in error "to the greatest possible misfortune of people whom we wish to save."[5] If a Christian makes erroneous arguments from Scripture on a matter that the unbelievers know

---

[5] See Appendix B for the full quotation from Augustine.

perfectly well, we should not expect them to believe the Scriptures on the more important matters of sin and salvation.

Even if the Bible is not discredited by its association with a faulty worldview, the advance of the gospel is hindered by the young earth worldview. Young earth creationism dams the rising tide of faith-affirming evidence for the Creator's handiwork. It is as though we have shut up the heavens and no longer allow them to tell anything more about the Creator's glory. God's eternal power and divine nature have been made evident through what has been made, but it apparently is clear and evident no more. Instead of tearing down the stronghold of naturalism and unbelief, the Perfect Paradise Paradigm forces us to lay down our swords.

I am therefore grateful that my pastor understood the significance of this issue when it was brought up by Dr. McLynn. More than simply seeking peace and averting a controversy, he realized that resolving the issue was important for helping our church to reach our city with the gospel of Christ. It was important enough that he assigned two senior associate pastors to continue meeting with us until we fully explored the creation controversy.

The Uncompromising Truths of Creation

Our series of meetings began predictably. The more vocal young earth proponent came out of the gate accusing us of not believing the Bible and denying the gospel. After spending the first two weeks listening to a one-sided monologue, the pastors—who knew us well enough to not believe the accusations—decided it was time to hear from us.

It had always been my opinion that the two camps agree on the most important issues and only disagree on secondary points. Although it is very important, the age of the earth is not a test of orthodoxy. So to defuse some of the tension and clear the confusion I decided to start building from a foundation of truth that we all held in common. Beginning with these shared, uncompromising truths of creation, it became clear where we agreed and exactly where we parted ways. What follows is a summary of this dialogue.

Common Ground

Truth #1: God has truthfully revealed Himself in many ways. Scripture clearly and repeatedly establishes the truth that the Creator has revealed Himself in many ways (Hebrews 1:1–2) and that His revelation is trustworthy (Titus 1:2; Psalm 119:160). His nature demands that all revelation, whatever the means, must be true and consistent.

There are important implications of this uncompromising truth. The fact that revelation must be interpreted means that there is potential for misunderstanding and disagreement.[6] But when properly applied, accurate science and sound theology should be consistent. When conflicts occur between science and theology, there is an opportunity for greater learning. Because God has revealed Himself in His word and in what He has made, science and theology are complementary tools in the pursuit of His truth.

Truth #2: The Creator is transcendent. With the first five simple words of Genesis, the Bible distinguishes itself from all other ancient literature. The phrase "In the beginning, God created . . ." immediately presumes that God has always existed. Moreover, these five words imply that what was created has not always existed. It is easy to miss the stark uniqueness of this passing pronouncement. This profound, naked assertion cuts across the grain of the science and philosophy of every other worldview

---

[6] Some will say that the Scripture provides a key to unlock the mysteries of science, but the unending disputes on matters large and small among theologians evidence the fact that biblical interpretation and systematic theology are difficult endeavors.

until the early twentieth century.[7] Matter, space, energy, and time have not always existed—but the Creator has. According to the Scriptures, there was a beginning, and there was a Creator.

Truth #3: The Creator is sovereign. The next five words of the Bible say, ". . . the heavens and the earth." This all-inclusive compound phrase asserts that everything that has been or ever will be is a direct or indirect result of God's original creation. The Creator who was there at the beginning exists wholly independent of the physical world that He created.

Interestingly, that is exactly what science tells us that nature reveals. Everything that exists—all of matter, space, energy and time—was brought into existence at a particular point in the past by an independent Agent. What does the Bible say? The Creator has the sovereign power to bring everything that exists into being: "In the beginning, God created the heavens and the earth."

It should be of no surprise that nature agrees with the Bible on the topic of creation. Notice that the first five words speak of His divine nature, and the second five speak of His eternal power. The Creator transcends the natural world, implying His supernatural or divine nature. The Creator brought everything into being from nothing, implying His eternal power. These two characteristics are exactly what Romans 1:20 says that the creation reveals.

Truth #4: The Creator is purposeful. Both camps agree on this point as well. God created all things because of His will to create. The Scripture repeatedly speaks of the Creator's eternal purpose. The act of creating the material world was but one step in what can be described as a drama, played out on the stage of this

---

[7] Albert Einstein forced his equations of general relativity to agree with his philosophy of an eternal "steady state" universe until he was persuaded that the universe is indeed expanding from a beginning. He could not avoid the implications of Edwin Hubble's astronomical data—that at a particular point in time a transcendent, supernatural cause brought everything into existence from nothing.

world. He created all things exactly as planned for a purpose, one that is greater even than the world itself.

Genesis 1 indicates that creation was a methodical process. The Creator systematically spoke and creation proceeded according to His direction. "God said . . . and it was so . . . and God saw that it was good . . . and there was evening and there was morning." After six days His creative work was completed, and He rested.

Moses penned the creation narrative under the inspiration of the Holy Spirit in a surprisingly succinct manner. Many questions would be more easily resolved if he had only elaborated. But in that succinctness is found a timeless narrative that has been approachable and understandable through the centuries. Less information would have made the divine revelation less remarkable. More information might have made the revelation less understandable.

More than just methodical, the purposeful nature of God is evident in the factual accuracy of the account. The contrast between the Genesis creation account and all other ancient creation accounts is nothing less than staggering. All other accounts are written in a very mystical and mythological fashion. They read more like fantasy tales than historical reality. But the Hebrew creation account is written in an almost documentary fashion. Perhaps most compelling of all is not what is written therein so much as what is absent. Having been educated in the palaces of Egypt, one would expect Egyptian science to penetrate the words of Genesis if it were authored solely by Moses. But instead, Moses wrote of a Creator that exists outside the bounds of space and time: One who brought all matter, energy, and time into existence at a single point in time. He providentially crafted the heavens and the earth and systematically created life. These were utterly foreign concepts to the Egyptians. The simple fact that Genesis does not contain the spurious science of Moses' day is strong evidence of divine authorship.

The Fork in the Road

Up to this point, the two parties were in agreement. The next point, however, is the fork in the road.

Truth #5: The original creation was very good. Our young earth creationist friends argue from this point that the original creation was a place with no suffering, no pain, and no death. From the presumption that the "very good" world was pristine and perfect in every way, the Perfect Paradise Paradigm reasons that there was no physical death before the fall, that the entire creation was radically refashioned after the fall and again during the flood, and that all physical evidence to the contrary is a consequence of a corrupted revelation.

But there is a better paradigm, one that recognizes the eternal purpose for creation, a purpose that will not be fully realized until the final consummation. The historical foundation of orthodox Christian theology is that this world was created with a specific end in view. In full anticipation of the unfolding drama of creation, this world was created with the ultimate end of glorifying the Creator. It was never intended to be a pristine paradise, a place of unblemished tranquility for man to enjoy forever. This world was created for a purpose, and it was perfectly suited to accomplish the Creator's perfect purpose. It was in light of that perfect, eternal purpose that the finished creation was declared "very good." But until the time our temporal, light afflictions give way to an eternal weight of glory, all creation groans with eager anticipation.

A Final Hope

I did not have a chance to follow up with Dr. McLynn after that Sunday evening class. Not long afterward she moved with her husband to another city. I would very much have liked to discuss the issues at greater length with her. Perhaps she would have reached the same conclusion as our two senior associate pastors after our series of weekly meetings. They concluded that nothing I taught was in conflict with sound doctrine, biblical authority, or biblical inerrancy. My old earth perspective certainly had not compromised the Bible or the nature of God. In fact, they came to see that this ancient creation paradigm holds a high view of the sovereignty of God and His eternal purpose for creation.

Perhaps someday Dr. McLynn and I will resume our conversation.

SUFFERING AND THE CHILD OF GOD

Christianity routinely approaches life from a paradoxical perspective. Jesus taught His followers that if someone slapped them on the cheek, they were to turn the other cheek and let them strike again. Likewise, if someone were to sue you for your shirt, you are to give your jacket as well. If someone forces you to go one mile, volunteer to go the second also. Jesus spoke of losing one's life in order to gain it and letting the dead bury the dead. It should be little surprise then that the Bible teaches us to exult in our tribulations. Paradoxical as it might be, this is the teaching of Jesus.

Why should there be tribulations in the lives of God's children? Are we simply to make the best of a bad situation? Far from it, the Bible teaches that suffering is often part of the fabric of this life. Even though we suffer, we can be confident that God loves us and has plans for our welfare. He is concerned about our daily lives; He is touched by our infirmities and indeed calls us to come before His throne where He provides grace in our time of need.

God With Us

The god that philosophers assume would prevent evil if able is not the God of the Bible. Nowhere does the Bible give the impression that God wants to alleviate all of our suffering and difficulties in this temporary life. Rather that preventing suffering, most examples in the Bible illustrate the opposite: God choosing not to remove or prevent suffering. At his conversion, Paul was told he would suffer. God had a great responsibility to give Paul, but it would come with a great price. He had to count the cost and choose to either be used by God in His kingdom or by Satan against God's kingdom. Later, Paul prayed and asked God three times to remove the torment caused by a messenger of Satan. God did not remove the thorn, but He did something better. He promised to be with him.

Most significant of all, Jesus prayed that the Father would remove the cup of suffering He was sent to endure, but to our great benefit the Father said no. It was God's will for the Son to suffer; indeed it pleased the Father to crush Him in order to complete the plan of redemption. If Jesus "learned obedience from the things which He suffered" (Hebrews 5:8), should the faithful child of God expect anything different?

On the eve of His crucifixion, Jesus spent considerable time in prayer. He prayed for the Father's glory to be revealed through Him as He completed His appointed work. He also interceded on behalf of those who had come to believe the Father's message, praying for their unity and their preservation. If there was ever an occasion for God the Son to express His intention of preventing suffering for His followers, this was it. Instead of asking for the prevention of suffering, He asked for their preservation from evil. He prayed, "I do not ask You to take them out of the world, but to keep them from the evil one" (John 17:15). This is the Biblical solution to the problem of suffering for the child of God. God does not promise to prevent difficulties but rather promises to be with us in the difficult times.

At every difficult juncture, God promises to be with His people. This is the consistent pattern demonstrated in the Bible. When the responsibility for leading God's people into the Promised Land was handed over to Joshua, he must have been shaking in his sandals. He had witnessed the capable leadership of Moses since the beginning of the Exodus, but now it was his turn. What was it that God told Joshua at this point of transition? God said, "Have I not commanded you? Be strong and courageous! Do not tremble or be dismayed, for the LORD your God is with you wherever you go" (Joshua 2:9). God took away the fear and apprehension by giving Joshua the assurance that He would be with him. To each believer, God gives the same encouragement to bear us up during difficult times:

> Do not fear, for I am with you;
> Do not anxiously look about you, for I am your God.
> I will strengthen you, surely I will help you,
> Surely I will uphold you with My righteous right hand. . . .
> When you pass through the waters, I will be with you;
> And through the rivers, they will not overflow you.
> When you walk through the fire, you will not be scorched,
> Nor will the flame burn you.
> For I am the LORD your God,
> The Holy One of Israel, your Savior. (Isaiah 41:10; 43:2–3)

When we pass through the rivers of turmoil in this life, God promises us that He will be with us. Sometimes He calms the storm, sometimes He lets us walk on the wind-driven waves, and sometimes we go down with the ship. But at each time of testing and trial we can be assured that God is with us.

Asaph, the psalmist, questioned the apparent inequity in life and how the righteous seemed to suffer even more than the wicked. Recording his thoughts in the seventy-third Psalm, he says:

> Surely God is good to Israel,
>   To those who are pure in heart!
> But as for me, my feet came close to stumbling,
>   My steps had almost slipped.

> For I was envious of the arrogant
> As I saw the prosperity of the wicked.
> For there are no pains in their death,
> And their body is fat.
> They are not in trouble as other men,
> Nor are they plagued like mankind.

Why is it that the righteous suffer when the wicked seem to have it so good? Asaph continued to elaborate on this quandary until he saw it from a different perspective.

> When I pondered to understand this,
> It was troublesome in my sight
> Until I came into the sanctuary of God;
> Then I perceived their end.

When he saw beyond the temporal experience of this life to view life from the perspective of the end, He had faith in God's purpose. It is only in light of the end that the present can make sense. He understood that God was in control, and God was on His side. All would be right in the end.

> Nevertheless I am continually with You;
> You have taken hold of my right hand.
> With Your counsel You will guide me,
> And afterward receive me to glory.

Having begun the psalm from the perspective of this world and questioning what God was allowing to happen, he concludes the psalm with a glorious statement of the believer's proper attitude toward difficulties in this life. He writes,

> Whom have I in heaven but You?
> And besides You, I desire nothing on earth.
> My flesh and my heart may fail,
> But God is the strength of my heart and my portion
> forever.
> For, behold, those who are far from You will perish;

You have destroyed all those who are unfaithful to You.
But as for me, the nearness of God is my good;
I have made the Lord GOD my refuge,
That I may tell of all Your works.

For the child of God, good is not defined by the absence of difficulties and sufferings. Goodness in this life is the nearness of God. He is our refuge, our help in times of trouble. He is our portion for this life; we need nothing more than His presence in our lives. And yet the presence of suffering helps us realize that this world is not all we need. It strips us of our desire for things on earth and uncovers an unwavering desire for God. Suffering uncovers the longing of our soul to be with our Creator and see the consummation of His glorious plan.

There is a deep, yet subtle significance to God's promise to be with us. God's promise to abide with us during suffering is an indication that we are partners in His unchanging, eternal plan. He doesn't begrudgingly bear us up during trials as if we are getting our due. Rather, it is the irony of God's perspective on good in the midst of sorrow that is striking. Good is not the absence of difficulties and suffering, but rather the faithful participation of His people in the outworking of His glorious eternal plan.

The suffering child of God can be comforted by the fact that God has a plan; God is with us when we suffer, and our suffering will eventually give way to glory. "'For I know the plans that I have for you,' declares the LORD, 'plans for welfare and not for calamity to give you a future and a hope'" (Jeremiah 29:11).

Suffering in the Will of God

Far from blaming all suffering on the sin of Adam, the Bible tells us that believers suffer according to the will of God (1 Peter 4:16). Temporal suffering accomplishes the Master's eternal purpose. God made both the day of blessing and the day of suffering according to His purposes: "In the day of prosperity be happy, but in the day of adversity consider—God has made the one as well as the other so that man will not discover anything that will be after him" (Ecclesiastes 7:14).

God permits suffering in the lives of His people for several reasons. First, suffering teaches us to depend on Him. This is the reason for Paul's suffering in 1 Corinthians 3. Paul also learned that God was with him all through his suffering (Philippians 4:11–13). The Psalmist declared that whatever happened, his times were in God's hands, and he would trust Him. His hope was that his life was part of the unfolding Master plan.

Second, God uses suffering to mature us and make us like Christ. Jesus matured through suffering, so we should expect no less. Since our highest end is to know God as we become more like Christ, suffering is essential to our Christian experience (John 17:3). To know through common experience pushes us to a more intimate level of knowledge than observation does. We know Him by sharing in His sufferings. Our sorrows should therefore be treasured rather than despised.

Appendix B
HUMILITY FROM HISTORY

History is replete with examples of sincere followers of Christ who seek to rightly divide the truth yet nonetheless err in interpretation. There have been many instances throughout history where the prevailing view of science has stood in opposition to mainstream biblical interpretations. In many instances theology was right, but in some significant instances science was correct. As early as the fourth century, Augustine understood the necessity of recognizing well-established scientific principles when interpreting difficult passages of Scripture. In *De Genese ad Litteram* Augustine says:

> It very often happens that there is some question as to the earth or the sky, or the other elements of this world—respecting which one who is not a Christian has knowledge derived from most certain reasoning or observation, and it is very disgraceful and mischievous and of all things to be carefully avoided, that a Christian speaking of such matters as being according to the Christian Scriptures, should be heard by an unbeliever talking such nonsense that the unbeliever perceiving him to be as wide of the mark as east from west, can hardly restrain himself from laughing.

And the real evil is not that a man is subjected to derision because of his error, but it is that to profane eyes, our authors (that is to say, the sacred authors) are regarded as having had such thoughts; and are also exposed to blame and scorn upon the score of ignorance, to the greatest possible misfortune of people whom we wish to save. For, in fine, these profane people happen upon a Christian busy in making mistakes on a subject which they know perfectly well; how, then, will they believe these holy books? How will they believe in the resurrection of the dead and in the hope of life eternal, and in the kingdom of heaven, when, according to an erroneous assumption, these books seem to them to have as their object those very things which they, the profane, by their direct experience or by calculation which admits of no doubt? It is impossible to say what vexation and sorrow prudent Christians meet with through these presumptuous and bold spirits who, taken to task one day for their silly and false opinion, and realizing themselves on the point of being convicted by men who are not obedient to the authority of our holy books, wish to defend their assertions so thoughtless, so bold, and so manifestly false. For they then commence to bring forward as a proof precisely our holy books, or again they attribute to them from memory that which seems to support their opinion, and they quote numerous passages, understanding neither the texts they quote, nor the subject about which they are making statement.

Yet Augustine himself was not immune to this error. In spite of solid evidence from science, Augustine fell victim to the very folly that he had warned of. He dismissed the idea of inhabitants on the other side of the earth as unscriptural:

But as to the fable that there are Antipodes, that is to say, men on the opposite side of the earth, where the sun rises when it sets to us, men who walk with their feet opposite ours, that is on no ground credible. . . . For Scripture, which proves the truth of its historical statements by the accomplishment of its prophecies, gives no false information; and it is too absurd to say, that some men might have taken ship and traversed the whole wide ocean, and crossed from this side of the world to the other, and that thus even the inhabitants of that distant region are descended from that one first man.[1]

Augustine thought he was using the Scriptures to demolish bad science, but in fact he was opposing good science with bad theology. True, Scripture certainly "gives no false information," yet we sometimes misinterpret the information given in the Scriptures. This is not to lessen the tremendous scholarship devoted to the correct interpretation of Scripture; it is simply to indicate that history demonstrates the wisdom of humility.

It is understandable that Augustine would make this mistake. And to be fair, Augustine was not opposing well-established science—the scientific consensus was still building at that time. But the lesson for us today is that we must not simply dismiss out-of-hand the weight of scientific evidence when it conflicts with our theological paradigms. We must test all things, even our theological paradigms. We should humbly recognize that although we think our interpretations are correct, our interpretations might need adjustment on occasion. Our interpretations may simply arise from what the Scripture appears to clearly say from our paradigm.

---

[1] Augustine, "The City of God," in *Nicene and Post-Nicene Fathers*, Eerdmans, Grand Rapids, 1956, vol. 2, p. 315.